"TICKETS, PLEASE..."

All About California Railroads

"TICKETS, PLEASE..."

All About California Railroads

By Dolan Eargle, Jr.

A California Living Book

First Edition

Copyright © 1979 California Living Books

The San Francisco Examiner Division of
The Hearst Corporation,
Suite 223, The Hearst Building,
Third and Market Streets,
San Francisco, California   94103

Printed in the United States of America.

ISBN 0-89395-012-2

Library of Congress Catalog Card Number 78-75156

Production by David Charlsen

Picture Sources:
California History Society
(pp. 11, 18, 20, 25, 34,
40, 65, 137, 147),
Southern Pacific,
California Western
Railroad, Associated Press,
Western Pacific, Sierra
Railroad, Amtrak, Dolan
Eargle, Jr., Disneyland,
Lion Country Safari,
Knott's Berry Farm.

Photographs on pages 16,
19, 24, 27, 30, 33, 40, 41,
49, 55, 91, 96, 107, 109,
115 copyright ©
Ted Streshinsky.

Cartography by
Julie Nunes

Table of Contents

Introduction

For me, it all started when I was four years old. My father hoisted me up into the cab of a hissing black giant, a locomotive on the relatively short, twenty-eight-mile-long Lancaster & Chester (South Carolina) Railroad. The owner of this road was the legendary Leroy Springs, of "Springmaid" fabrics. Springs was known to frequent meetings of railroad barons, where his presence drew many snide remarks. Allegedly, he waved them off with, "My railroad might not be as long as yours, but it's just as wide!" A true railfan.

Powerful impressions made early in life that are repeated periodically are often highly influential in setting the direction of later energies. To live next to a railroad for years, as I did; to ride streetcars as a diversion, as I did; to make long rail journeys occasionally, as I did — are experiences that provide strong reasons for becoming a railfan. These experiences are, at first, part entertainment, part necessity for transportation, and part environmental. But subtly, over time, the fascination with trains for their own sake takes over.

Several years ago, as a newcomer to San Francisco, while out on a Sunday drive, I spotted the distant but unmistakable outlines of big, black locomotives parked in a field near the Richmond Bridge. I was in ecstasy! I *had* to get closer. The fact that I had to unravel the maze of roads to reach the site only heightened my excitement. At last, I found the Castro Point Railway's shops, yards, and yes, even the hissing black giants like those I'd known as a child. The experience was every bit as wonderful as I'd hoped.

I wanted to explore more of California's railroad treasures. How could I find them? Alas, no rail guide existed — so it was up to me. I then started my campaign of tracking down tracks.

I'm well aware that some of you may find all this railroad interest prosaic, just another way to get from here to there. But I suspect that deep down, everyone is moved and exhilarated by a train's click-clack, its gentle sway, its straining motor moving tons in a smooth glide.

For a long time, I thought it was enough to enthusiastically accept whatever rail adventure happened by. But eventually I stopped being a passive passenger and deliberately set out to find "new" railroads. I wanted to experience that sense of history, that fragrance of nostalgia, that great, mechanical power that moves tons of weight so sleekly.

Ever since Peter Cooper put his "Tom Thumb" on two bands of steel in Baltimore in 1830, railroads have fascinated the nation. For some people, railroads — with their hissing, their belching smoke, their screeching motors and engines, their awesome controlled power, and their huge parts moving right in front of our eyes — appeal to *all* the senses. Trucks, buses, boats, and planes, with their covered out-of-sight motors, can go almost anywhere and be seen everywhere. But a train is almost a rarity: it is constrained to move neatly on a pre-set course. Why do we get such a kick out of model trains? Maybe because they go only where *we* want them to, not willy-nilly over house or yard.

What can be said about the person with that inexplicable zeal to seek out yet another rail experience — the choo-choo junkie? For me, as for most railfans, the real reason cannot be pinned down or explained. I only know that some strange drive impels me to search for a new set of tracks to marvel over.

Recently I visited the California Railroad Museum near Rio Vista. The yards were crawling with people, all dedicated to restoring and noting every detail of old locomotives and interurban trains. I spent quite a few hours there, chatting with the other aficionados — and in all that time, not one of us questioned *why* we were interested in this particular antique mania.

Railroads have always had a spotted reputation. They have made both covert and ill-concealed demands on the public and its treasury. Their leaders have more often than not been greedy and insensitive. In spite of all this, the same put-upon public still appreciates that railroads are necessary — and more, that they beckon our sense of adventure, that they don't simply transport us and our goods but also offer us a delighted state of mind. Not long ago, Senator Lowell Weickert of Connecticut defended assaults on Amtrak by saying, "Rails are an idea whose time has come." Let's hope so.

A few words about this guidebook: initially, I set out to explore the railroads of California, both past and present, for my sake only; but after I made a few discoveries, I realized that this information should be shared with other railfans, both present and future. Although the act of searching out these railroads is great sport in itself, it's helpful to have some sort of guide to start off with — especially for those who are unfamiliar with California railroading.

This guide is intended for both the casual railrider and the serious railfan. Recreational railriders will find within these pages something to ride or to observe in almost every part of the state. And although many experienced students of railroads probably already know about most of the information contained here, they still may find useful the new information on the up-to-date holdings and status of some lines.

Part of my purpose here, as with all guidebooks, is to help the reader enjoy the many facets of railroading more fully. To that end, I have abbreviated many histories, accounts, and even schedules and fares. Those of you who want to examine these subjects in further detail might search out more particulars on the site itself, consult several of the books and publications listed in the bibliography, or pay a visit to some of the bookstores listed.

Even over the short period of time that exists between this writing and your reading, some change is inevitable. Although all the schedules, fares, and equipment holdings given here are as up-to-date as possible as of mid-1978, they are, of course, subject to change. For any number of reasons, including withering insurance rates, excursion lines and some miniatures may partially or totally cease operations overnight. And since railroad engines and cars are highly mobile, and since they constantly are being bought, sold, and transferred, they just might not be found at the sites reported in this guide.

The information you find here comes from a large variety of sources — personal observation, some remarkable books, pamphlets, booklets, brochures, and maps; and interviews with railroad personnel, from official representatives to trackworkers. In my desire to make this guide as historically accurate as possible, I have tried to cross-check all data; but since occasionally I have had to rely solely upon the (sometimes fallible) memory of various human beings, there may be a few errors or tall tales.

I know that there must be things I have missed; I suspect that some factual mistakes have crept in. Therefore, I would be pleased if the many knowledgeable railfans reading this guide would "blow the whistle" on me and help correct and amend the data for future editions.

So for all of you who wish to experience the pleasure of riding over steel rails on steel wheels, and for those of you who are interested in a rich and complex aspect of California's historical past, present, and future — welcome aboard!

Dolan H. Eargle, Jr.
San Francisco, 1978

PART I
A BRIEF HISTORY OF RAILROADS IN CALIFORNIA

Getting Established (1850s-1870s)

In the mid-nineteenth century, California was noisy, violent, and bustling with activity. The inrush of miners, settlers, and fortune seekers that overflowed California after the Mexican War of 1848, the Gold Rush of 1849, and the acqusition of statehood in 1850 caused the most feverish development the state has ever experienced.

Primitive trails became roads, rivers became arteries, and railroads became the prime movers of people and commerce. Within only fifteen years after introducing its first railroad engine in 1855, San Francisco was the western base of the first transcontinental railroad, as well as of a multitude of smaller railroads clustered about the two large population centers — San Francisco and Sacramento.

Every time the north wind blew, the sands of San Francisco shifted. That sand had to be moved — in the wake of the population influx of the early 1850s, new construction in the impatient city couldn't wait. To accomplish this gritty task, California's first steam engine, the "Elephant," was shipped around Cape Horn in 1855, along with a few rails.

The "Elephant" was one of those engines that model builders like to imitate because it represents locomotives of the Civil-War era — huge, diamond-shaped smokestacks; five-foot driving wheels; headlamps the size of restaurant mixing bowls; and wooden pilots ("cowcatchers") like snowplows. This style can still be seen in the miniatures of the Kennedy Park Express in Hayward, the coal-fired "Nevada" of the Folsom Valley Railroad, and the full-sized narrow gauges of Disneyland.

Once the "Elephant" had fulfilled its sand-shifting mission, it was redubbed the "C.K. Garrison," and it soon became one of the four locomotives of California's first commercial rail line, the Sacramento Valley Railroad. This forty-mile pioneer, extending from Sacramento to Folsom, was engineered by Theodore D. Judah, who today is memorialized by a plaque in Sacramento and by both a street and a streetcar line in San Francisco.

Why were the two towns of Sacramento and Folsom chosen to be termini of the first railroads? Sacramento's claim was that it was the head of navigation on the rivers flowing from the gold fields. Every day, pioneers, miners, and immigrants were arriving by the boatload; the new farmland had to be provisioned and its produce hauled to market; and heavy equipment for the gold mines had to be brought in.

And Folsom, a bustling trade center on the American River at the edge of the Central Valley, like any town with aspirations of growth, sought — and got — a railroad.

Before long, most of the new little towns along the Sierra foothills were clamoring for a railroad to move their people and produce in and out. The wagon roads flooded each winter, and except for railroads, wagons provided the only way to move heavy freight. But railroads were more than just a backup for wagons; they were cheaper, too, charging about 4¢ a ton-mile. Even mule skinners charged upwards of $1.

Soon, there were other railroads. Within six years, the San Francisco-Sacramento region blossomed with short lines like the San Francisco & San Jose Railroad (1864), the Alameda Valley Railroad, and the San Francisco & Oakland Railroad (the latter two were Oakland port lines that also were established in 1864). At the same time, connecting lines were expanding the network: the California Central Railroad (1862) stretched the track from Folsom to Lincoln, and the Sacramento, Placer, & Nevada Railroad (1862) extended it from Folsom to Auburn.

Some of these active little towns were thinking beyond their own local affairs, and hoping — and often scheming — to couple their local lines to a transcontinental railroad. Much of the local bustle was strictly regional, but across the state and nation larger things were stirring.

The largest of these was the Civil War. Both Congress and President Lincoln were easily persuaded that the West must be tied to the East, and quickly. Therefore, the Pacific Railway Act was signed in July 1862, at a time when the war was not going well for the Union, and when the Union, needing all the material and voter support it could get, felt it expedient to yield to California's demands for recognition from Washington.

As with most projects of that precarious era, once the decision had been made, the petty bickering began. Where was the railroad to be routed?

As early as 1853, Congress had paid Mexico $10 million for the Gadsden Purchase — desert land that would ensure an all-weather route, one that could be used year round. In an age when wood was needed to fuel steam-boiler engines and for construction materials, however, this dry, unproductive region was hardly satisfactory. Interest in heavily forested Northern California proved stronger.

Theodore Judah had contemplated the two routes. One would go through Dutch Flat (roughly paralleling today's Interstate Highway 80) using his Sacramento Valley Railroad and possibly the Sacramento, Placer & Nevada RR. The other would pass through Placerville (following the route of the modern U.S. Highway 50).

Four foresighted — but not notably altruistic — petty businessmen from Sacramento were captivated by Judah's northern-route plan: Leland Stanford, Collis P. Huntington, Charles Crocker, and Mark Hopkins. Later, they became known as the "Big Four" and the "Associates," as well as by other, less exalted, terms.

In 1861, the four formed the Central Pacific Railroad, and with the prospect of receiving federal grant support through the Pacific Railway Act, they began their march eastward to fame and fortune. By hook and crook, they outmaneuvered the efforts of all rivals to gain "their" route over the Sierras — the Dutch Flat-Donner Summit passage. And only thirty-nine years after the first, primitive railroad was built in the U.S., the phenomenal, splendid, and fully developed Central Pacific joined the Union Pacific at Promontory Point, Utah, in May 1869.

A Concord-type stagecoach and Central Pacific locomotive at the railhead at Cisco in the Sierra Nevada Mountains of California, 1867.

California's Interstate Railroad Routes

Central Pacific (SP)	1869	Sacramento (Ca.), Donner Summit (Ca.), Reno (Nev.)
Southern Pacific (Sunset Route)	1882	Los Angeles (Ca.), San Bernardino (Ca.), Yuma (Ariz.)
Nevada, California, & Oregon	1882	Lakeview (Ore.), Alturas (Ca.), Reno (Nev.) [transcontinental connections to Klamath Falls (Ore.) by SP, 1927]
Carson & Colorado	1883 (-1960)	Owens Vly., Reno area (SP-owned, 1900)
Atchison, Topeka, & Santa Fe	1885	San Diego (Ca.), Cajon Pass (Ca.), Barstow (Ca.), Needles (Ca.), Salt Lake City (Ut.) (Barstow-Needles built by SP, 1883)
Central Pacific (SP) (Siskiyou line)	1887	The Central Valley (Ca.), Redding (Ca.), Ashland (Ore.)
Great Northern (BN)	1893	Bieber (Ca.), Klamath Falls (Ore.)
Union Pacific (Salt Lake Route)	1905	Los Angeles (Ca.), Cajon Pass (Ca.), Barstow (Ca.), Las Vegas (Nev.) (built by San Pedro, Los Angeles & Salt Lake RR; UP-owned, 1921)
Tonopah & Tidewater	1907 (-1940)	Ludlow (Ca.), Beatty (Nev.)
Southern Pacific (Cascade line)	1909	Weed (Ca.), Klamath Falls (Ore.)
Western Pacific (Feather River Route)	1910	Oakland (Ca.), Sacramento (Ca.), Oroville (Ca.), Salt Lake City (Ut.)
Atchison, Topeka, & Santa Fe	1910	Cadiz (on Barstow-Needles line), Parker and Phoenix (Ariz.)
San Diego & Arizona Eastern	1919	San Diego (Ca.), El Centro (Ca.)

THE NEW STREAMLINER "CITY OF SAN FRANCISCO"

Railroads Rampant (1860s-Early 1900s)

Rise of the Big Transcontinentals

Just about everyone has heard of the famous "Golden Spike" ceremony of 1869. Leland Stanford took the first swing – and missed. The remaining three of the "Big Four" then took turns, and – whether out of clumsiness, deference, or toadiness – also missed. Consequently, before the last golden spike was pounded into a crosstie to celebrate the completion of the first transcontinental railroad, it was thoroughly mauled.

Now that the stage was set, what would the railroad's performance be like?

Over the next forty years, California became a free-for-all for the railroad companies – especially for a well-capitalized and daring few. Their plans and constructions ruled all corners of the state and all facets of life, as we shall see.

The Big Four's Central Pacific-Southern Pacific complex was at the forefront of this race, with the Santa Fe, the Union Pacific, and the Spreckels' roads (see pp. 17, 18, and 20) driving the fiercest competition. Anyone who wants to learn more about the scandals associated with this tumultuous era can refer to Frank Norris' acrid 1901 novel, The Octopus.

California's extraordinarily rapid growth tempted many excited investors to try their hand at smaller railroading ventures. Most of these, however, were swallowed up by the giants' voracious appetites. "Build" and "merge" were the orders of the day.

Being the first in the business helped, but largely it was clever construction choices, shrewd takeovers, and unscrupulous business and political shenanigans that kept the CP-SP on top.

The job is done! On May 10, 1869, the locomotives of the Central Pacific (now Southern Pacific) and the Union Pacific met at Promontory Point, Utah, where the last spike was pounded in.

The Southern Pacific

The Southern Pacific[1] first arose as an independent owner of a projected southern route from San Jose through the Central Valley to Mojave. Recognizing the importance of this route, the Big Four bought it, its name, and its rights. In 1877, they constructed a line (now the Sunset Route) to Yuma, Arizona in one direction. Then they bought the existing San Francisco & San Jose RR to San Francisco, and tied it to the first line in the other direction.

Meanwhile, Stanford's SP was building yet another line toward the Atlantic & Pacific Railroad at Needles, which was completed in 1883. In 1885, to no one's great surprise, the enterprises *all* became known as the "Southern Pacific."

In the north, the Central Pacific assured itself a route out of California by purchasing the California & Oregon Railroad in 1868 and completing the road (the present Siskiyou line) in 1887. A second route (the Cascade line) followed in 1909. Both connected with transmountain routes in Oregon.

To ward off competition that threatened to move down the Owens Valley from Reno, a particularly easy end run around the Sierras to Los Angeles, the SP waged a short rate-war with the Los Angeles & Independence Railroad — and won. Now that it had made connection with the narrow gauge Carson & Colorado Railroad (see p. 124) tracks at Owenyo in 1910, the SP had the Owens Valley route sewed up. Eventually (in 1900), the C&C had to sell out to the SP, and the SP carried on this narrow-gauge interstate operation for fifty-nine years, connecting at the north end with the old Central Pacific (SP) transcontinental route just east of Sparks, Nevada.[2]

The Santa Fe

While the SP was attempting to secure a monopoly, other railroad interests were stirring — among them, the Atchison, Topeka, & Santa Fe Railway. By offering competition and, usually, lower rates, the AT&SF managed to win some respect from a populace that had been agitated by the SP's unprincipled practices. By threatening to snatch trade from the SP — in the form of a line to Guaymas, Mexico — the AT&SF forced the SP to sell them its Mojave-Needles line in 1884. Heeding San Diego's pleas for a railroad to service its excellent port, the Santa Fe (as the California Southern Railroad) reached there in 1885, once more connecting the Pacific Ocean with the East, and forcing the SP from its transcontinental monopoly.

Once it had established itself in California, the Santa Fe continued to expand. San Diego, Riverside, Los Angeles, and Orange Counties, all growing in agricultural production, benefited from the prodigious network of the railroad's branch lines. When the Santa Fe bought up the Spreckels' San Francisco & San Joaquin Valley Railroad in 1898, the Central Valley counties likewise found life easier — freight rates were now lower, and transcontinental markets were now available. This line, crisscrossing the SP's valley route several times, was the SP's primary competition in that area, and became the Santa Fe's main line to San Francisco. Freight moved *via* Richmond on the famous railroad barges to Fisherman's Wharf and China Basin; passengers, on the other hand, detrained in the East Bay and completed their journey to San Francisco by boat, making use of the SP ferry monopoly.

---

[1]Now known as the Southern Pacific Transportation Company.

[2]The SP's standard gauge portion from Mojave to Lone Pine remains.

The Union Pacific

Another route through the Mojave Desert threatened SP supremacy. Jay ("I don't build railroads. I buy them") Gould maneuvered frantically to achieve Union Pacific control over the SP. And he actually succeeded, for a short time (1901-1911); but after ten years, the UP was forced by antitrust action to withdraw. Nevertheless, through the finely tuned game of corporate struggle, the UP acquired the route of the San Pedro, Los Angeles, & Salt Lake Railroad. This had been built in 1905, and in 1921 it became another of the transcontinental railroads, crossing the California state line near Las Vegas.

The UP is Southern California's route from Los Angeles Harbor through Las Vegas to Salt Lake City and beyond. I say "beyond," for the UP has many more lines than just its one into California. Its primary influence lies in regions from Nevada and Oregon to Utah and eastward. Although the UP was Central Pacific's "end of track" at Promontory Point, Utah, when the first transcontinental line was completed in 1869, the SP was eventually given that portion of the line into Ogden, Utah.

The Western Pacific

The latest of the big transcontinental railroads to be established in California is the Western Pacific,[3] whose rails were completed in 1909 over the "Feather River Route." This extraordinarily scenic route, utilizing only a 1-percent grade over the Sierra from Oroville through Portola and Beckwourth Pass, was once familiar to the many Californians who enjoyed riding the "California Zephyr" from San Francisco-Oakland to Salt Lake City.

As recently as 1931, a rather odd time to be *building* railroads, the WP expanded northward from Keddie, on the North Fork of the Feather River, to a connection with the Burlington Northern RR (see p. 18) and the McCloud River RR (see p. 56). This connection, which passes through some of the most spectacular country in the Northern Sierra range, allows through trains of the BN and WP to reach port facilities in Stockton and Oakland (and San Francisco, via California's only remaining railferry. See p. 83).

The WP had also expanded by absorbing short lines near it, such as the Sacramento Northern (Concord-Sacramento-Marysville) and the Tidewater Southern (Stockton-Turlock).

[3]This was the second California railroad of that name. The first Western Pacific from San Jose to Sacramento was gobbled up by the Central Pacific in 1869.

Southern Pacific's No. 1 "C.P. Huntington" woodburner of the 1860s and an up-to-date diesel of 1955.

The Burlington Northern

Some time around 1893, the Great Northern Railroad, wanting to cash in on California's wealth, ran a road in as far north as Bieber in Lassen County. Later, this line connected with the WP there; northward, it forms the "Inside Gateway" trans-Sierra route (through Oregon) from California.

Although it came to California relatively late, the Burlington Northern Railroad grew really big just to the north. It is actually the product of a three-way merger: Minnesota magnate Jim Hill's Northern Pacific; the Great Northern; and the Chicago, Burlington, & Quincy. This fusion enabled the BN to control at least three transcontinental routes in Oregon and Washington, as well as the majority of all routes in the entire Northwest.

The first railroad ride in California, 1856, on the Sacramento Valley Railroad built by Theodore D. Judah.

Three Other Important Lines

There are three other railroads that, although not transcontinental, were significant in their connection to interstate or transcontinental lines.

The Nevada, California, & Oregon Railroad

In the far northeastern corner of California lies the route of one other trans-Sierra railroad, the Nevada, California, & Oregon. It began in 1882 as a narrow gauge, and it ended as a standard gauge, as part of two other transcontinental railroads. The NCO was rather unusual in that it ran from desert Reno through Northeastern California to forested Lakeview, Oregon without a tunnel, major bridge, or high summit crossing. But neither did it have one major industry along its entire 275 miles; and in the absence of business from industry, the railroad was forced to sell out.

The WP picked up the southern tail-end in 1918, as an access to Reno; the SP adopted the entire northern end in 1927, with a northern (Modoc) extension into Klamath Falls and a southern one to the old Central Pacific route. This addition gave the SP one more trans-Sierra route.

The San Diego & Arizona Eastern Railroad

In the far southwestern corner of the state, San Diego profited from the most recent of the eastern-bound connections, the San Diego & Arizona Eastern Railroad, built by John D. Spreckels in 1919. Mexican President Porfirio Diaz had agreed to let Spreckels choose the easiest route through the Coast Range, which meant using some forty-five miles of Mexican right-of-way from Tijuana to Tecate (see p. 138). For years, the ubiquitous SP had control of this remarkable railroad, but it is now owned by the city of San Diego.

The Tonopah & Tidewater Railroad

It wasn't really a transcontinental, but it was an interstate road, and it made connections on both ends with roads that were (and are) transcontinental. I'm speaking of the Tonopah & Tidewater Railroad, a charming, 170-mile, standard-gauge line that once ran from a junction of the Las Vegas & Tonopah Railroad in Beatty, Nevada, to Ludlow, California, east of Barstow, where it met the AT&SF. From 1907-1940, it existed to serve the many mines of the Eastern California desert region and the thousands of people who lived there and worked the mines. When the mines played out, so did the T&T.

The T&T's largest feeder line was the U.S. Borax Company's three-foot-gauge Death Valley Railroad (see p. 27), which in turn was fed by the company's two-foot "Baby Gauge" trains.[4]

---

[4]The DVRR's handsome engine #2 and a Baby Gauge engine are now on display at the U.S. Borax's Furnace Creek Ranch at the Death Valley National Monument Visitor Center.

Consequences of Unrestrained Expansion

As the construction and expansion of railroads boomed throughout California, and as the battle of the giants raged, the railroad users and the taxpayers began to agonize. Both pocketbooks and the public treasury were being thinned at an alarming rate. Obtaining the government subsidies and rate gouging became a way of life for the big companies.

If you wanted to promote a railroad 120 years ago — and if you had dreams, ambitions, and wealthy, influential friends, about all you had to do was simply announce your intentions and then sell stock to your influential friends and to the gullible public. Then, with the money (seldom enough) and ballyhoo this ploy brought in, you bought some right-of-way, some rails and ties, and an engine or two; and, using disillusioned miners as your labor force, you began building.

People seemed to enjoy working on the early railroads even though the working conditions were often atrocious.

Misuse of Subsidies and Rates

Many early railroaders were able to garner one other helpful item: a local, state, or federal subsidy. After all, didn't the populace need more and better transportation? And wasn't government supposed to help the public get what it needed?

For the larger, more powerful roads, the subsidy usually consisted of enormously generous land grants that had been engineered by the railroad lobby in governmental centers. Such grants gave the railroad outright ownership of the land alongside the right-of-way, which often extended in checkerboard fashion tens of miles on both sides of the road. Although the rights-of-way were especially wide where timber for fuel, crossties, and trestles were plentiful, it was uncommon to have more than 640 acres per mile of track.

In return, the government received either free toll or 50-percent reductions on its own mail, passenger, military, and freight traffic until 1940. Thereafter, more "just" rates were put into effect. Still, it has been estimated (based on a comparison of current land values with hauling rates) that the federal government got back several times its investment.

Frequently, interested citizens formed the backbone of local subsidies by subscribing their stocks, bonds, cash, or land if the railroad would only deign to locate its tracks through their town.

Once the tracks were down and the trains were running, rate wars broke out. Where there was no competition to keep the prices within reason, the prevailing dogma was to "charge what traffic will bear" rather than to base charges on operating costs plus a profit margin. For instance, in 1860, merchants complained that it cost less to ship a barrel of flour from Sacramento, California to Liverpool, England than it did to the Mother Lode counties, less than 150 miles away.

Where there *was* competition, fares did come down for a while. One contest was between SP's Central Valley route and the Spreckels Sugar family's San Francisco & San Joaquin Valley RR (which became Santa Fe's valley route in 1898). On some long hauls, some fares became ridiculously low. For example, in 1885, the SP charged $70 for passage from Kansas City to Los Angeles; but within four months after a war with the Santa Fe, the SP's fares were down to $2.50.

The giants had marked their territories, however; collusion began behind the scenes, and the rate seesaw went up again. Low rates were obtainable through kickbacks to the railroad or by exclusive contracts with (later illegal) rebates.

This locomotive, the "Governor Stanford," was built in the East and shipped around Cape Horn. Its first trip for Central Pacific was made at Sacramento on November 10, 1863.

Misuse of Labor--The Human Cost

How often we view a complete engineering feat, wonder at its functioning, and enjoy the fruits of its construction — without knowing of (or caring about) the great expenditure of human lives and values that went into its building. During this era, the railroad companies were among the worst exploiters of human toil.

People who travel on Interstate 80 over the Donner Pass, especially in winter, seldom fail to notice the long, thin stripe of the Southern Pacific tracks and snow sheds on the far side of the valley above Donner Lake. One hundred and ten years ago, the task of carving this spectacular railroad was given to Charles Crocker, chief of Central Pacific construction.

Crocker surveyed the labor market and found that, by coaxing Chinese from their homeland, he could save CP $4 per month per worker. Instead of paying whites $30 a month, he could pay the Chinese only $26.

The gutsy little Pacific Coast narrow-gauge railroad (see p. 30) that wound from San Luis Obispo to the hills south of Santa Maria got a similar "deal" — $1.15 a day for Chinese labor as opposed to $2.25 a day for white labor.

We marvel at the once-splendid network of Los Angeles' Pacific Electric interurban lines, built by an SP subsidiary. Those lines were built by Mexicans, at $1.50-1.75 a day, compared with the Anglo labor available at $2.50-3.00 a day.

Safety procedures were not used — in fact, they were practically unknown. Many tens of thousands of lives were lost in the process of building California's railroads.

But construction was not the only risky phase of railroading. The railroad car coupler, which we now take for granted, was invented by Eli Janney in 1873 (see p. 44). Today, this device seems simple enough; but back then, a dangerous, antique car-coupling method continued to be used for many years, due to inaction of the railroad managements. In 1881 alone, 30,000 brakemen across the nation lost their hands or their lives.

This photo, taken in the Sierra in 1877, shows an early timber trestle and embankment being built by Chinese workmen using only hand tools and one-horse dump carts — an amazing achievement.

Favorable Effects and External Problems

Railroads have always had their proponents and their adversaries, their shining moments and their dishonorable ones. Their accomplishments have been memorable, often exceptional; but their methods were often mischievous, if not downright villainous.

The rate wars of the 1880s certainly did no harm to the settling of California. Some of the huge land grant tracts were sold to the very settlers, developers, and speculators whom the railroads had attracted. The Central Pacific had received 1,349,000 acres, and its temptingly low rates brought in thousands of settlers from abroad and from struggling farms in the East and Midwest. For years, fertile land went for as little as 50¢ an acre.

There is no doubt that the success of the railroads and the growth of California during this era were due to a symbiotic union. California was now a firm part of the United States, and its railroads held sway in the nation as the conveyers of its produce, cattle, and industry.

The railroads had plenty of problems — and not all of them were entirely of their own making.

Weather was always a violent and ungovernable factor. Repeated washouts on the AT&SF main line in the Temecula Canyon of San Diego County forced that line to be severely rerouted in 1888. Heavy snows in the Sierra range constantly blocked the transcontinental routes in winter. Trestles were subject to flood, rot, and insects. Costs of rail upkeep were (and are still) high, and when rails were not serviced, they often failed. In consequence, some trains were "grounded."

The railroad companies also had to cope with the price of materials. Somehow, the San Francisco & San Jose RR of 1864 had procured locomotives for only about $15,000 each. Yet the Central Pacific had to pay $120,000 for some of its locomotives (although they *were* larger and more powerful) in the inflationary period toward the end of the Civil War.

The railroads were no more immune than any other companies to the financial recessions ("panics") of the era — notably those of 1875, 1893, and 1907.

To survive in those times, drastic cutbacks were called for. Reverberating throughout the industry were the disastrous effects of these cutbacks on labor, especially since labor was attempting simultaneous reforms of working conditions and wage rates, as we shall see.

Built in 1884, the "Sequoia," No. 3 of the California Western Railroad, arrived in Fort Bragg by ship.

Curbing the Giants (1880s-Early 1900s)

Reform and Control

Clearly, it was time to correct the abuses and restrain the power of the railroads. But most of the companies did not welcome suggestions of reform, and countered with their most powerful weapon — money. As Stuart Daggett wrote, "The associates met the proposal of government regulation as a threat to rob them of their property and resisted it as they would have opposed any other attack. . . . They frankly defended the use of money as a method of persuading men to do what was right."[1]

But the public protested, and in consequence, regulatory commissions such as the first California Railroad Commission of 1879, were set up. The railroads, however, did not accede gracefully. They struck back, using outright bribery, or — if that didn't work, packing the commission or the state legislature. The United States Railway Commission found that, in 1884 alone, the Central Pacific had managed to put some $600,000 into lobbying and bribery.

In another tactic, Crocker warned Placerville that he would halt construction on a new line if it didn't cool its anti-SP sentiments.

Finally, both the public and the press grew so incensed at the railroads' response to being regulated that they bore down upon the large railroad companies.

The public of that day really needed the railroads. Nearly all long-distance passenger traffic went by rail, and nearly all freight was moved by rail. Consequently, the railroads, more than other companies (e.g., manufacturers) that were less directly subject to public opinion, were always in the public eye. Thus they felt at least some necessity to defend their position publicly — and to mold public opinion in the press, if possible.

However, the press was not always on the side of the railroad barons, particularly when local issues were involved. For instance, in 1895 the San Francisco *Examiner,* encouraging competition against the Central Pacific monopoly in hopes of bringing down the high freight rates, offered gold watches to anyone who formed a stockholding club in any of the small towns along the route of the San Francisco & San Joaquin Valley RR — the CP's first big rival.

Reform from within also intensified during this era. After some initial struggles, the railroad brotherhoods were pretty effective in encouraging the reform and control of operating conditions. And reform was sorely needed — the early years of railroading were hell for the workmen. Wages were poor, the equipment was often shoddy and makeshift, the weather was fickle and dangerous. During the recession of 1875, the big companies cut wages so much that by 1877, a huge, violent, national strike broke out in Maryland and soon spread to San Francisco. One hundred men were left dead in its wake. Eventually the strike was broken; but the unions were solidified, and strife between railroad labor and management was never that intense again.

In 1894, Sacramento became enmeshed in the general strike that originated at the Pullman Company in Chicago. Several persons were killed in rioting, and an SP train was wrecked near Davis. Public and press feeling against this kind of union-inspired violence ran so high that California enacted a law that considered causing death by train wreck a capital offense. This law stayed on the books until the 1970s.

At that time (as now), local communities were sympathetic to labor's efforts to improve its circumstances. In 1907, San Francisco's municipal lines struck for a 2¢ per hour increase, an eight-hour day, and a daily wage of $3. But riots followed the strike, and three people died.

[1]Stuart Daggett, *Chapters on the History of the Southern Pacific* (New York: Ronald Press Co., 1922).

Since these struggles, however, management has tended to be more responsive to labor's legitimate demands; and violence in strikes, whether bred by management minions or frustrated workers, has greatly diminished.

The last decades of the century were characterized by a rising anti-railroad feeling in the legislature and the courts, as the public became aware of the railroads' abuses, and as reform-minded politicians were brought to power.

Also, as new railroads sprang up, providing a breath of healthy competition, and as Stanford, Crocker, Huntington, and Hopkins (the "Big Four") died, some of the concentrated power began to diminish. Rivalries among northern, central, and southern companies in California brought forth some new roads. Newer, somewhat more responsive and responsible heads came to power — E. H. Harriman (UP) and Edward Ripley (AT&SF) — and much of the baronial railroading of former years was transformed into a more subdued, modern-style corporate capering.

By the end of the early 1900s, with the advent of national control by the Interstate Commerce Commission of 1888, the Railroad Commission Act of 1911, and the Transportation Act of 1920, the railroads were under weighty regulation. The public left the railroads to government regulation and turned its attention to the abuses perpetrated by other kinds of corporate entities, such as oil and utilities.

A narrow-gauge railroad that fed into a larger line crosses a spidery trestle in Nevada County, the Sierra foothills.

The Rise and Demise of Several Short Lines

The big roads put their lines through from city to city, choosing routes where they could pick up the largest amount of freight and passenger business, or where future development looked most promising. Sometimes a route was dictated by the terrain. The small town that couldn't raise the interest of a planning engineer, or that found itself in some remote corner, quickly got worried about its future existence.

Such was the plight of Shasta City, a mountain town that was separated by both horizontal and vertical miles from the main SP line to Oregon. Today, it lies deserted and in ruins. The more fortunate town of Redding connected with that line instead. Yreka, Quincy, and Santa Maria also found themselves some distance from the main lines; but they were able to build their own railroads, which survive today, and the towns prospered then, as now. Towns like these adopted the slogan that the Bath & Hammondsport (NY) Railroad originated: "A Short Line is a Hell of a Lot Better Than No Line."

Other towns built a railroad and prospered for a while, but then woke up one day to find that their trains — usually used in connection with lumbering or mining — were no longer needed.

Lumbering often provides only an impermanent livelihood, especially if the loggers have been hasty or greedy. Consider Bella Vista in Shasta County. Once it was a thriving lumbering town; now it is merely a quiet intersection on a dry, oak-studded plain. In 1926, the pastoral hush was broken by the occasional whistle of mixed trains of the California, Shasta & Eastern Railroad that ran from the Terry Lumber Company flume in Bella Vista to the SP connection in Anderson. But over the years, the timber thinned, and the company overextended itself and — along with its railroad — went broke. Today, nature is slowly reclaiming the few remaining crossties in the fields alongside Deschutes Road, as well as the three, castle-like bridge piers in the Sacramento River. Most of the region's irrigation water flows away to the more fertile south before being put to crops.

The mining town has always had a precarious existence. The extent of a lode, a vein, or a deposit is seldom truly known. When the silver and borax mines of Calico (San Bernardino County) and the mercury mines of New Almaden (near Los Gatos in Santa Clara County) gave out, the loss of the railroads was near at hand. Eventually, Calico lost its Waterloo Mining Company railroad (see p. 118), and Los Gatos saw the last train of the South Pacific Coast Railroad (also a passenger line) close down one afternoon at 5:37 P.M. In memory of the South Pacific Coast, the current Billy Jones Wildcat Railroad in Los Gatos closes down at 5:37 P.M. each day. (See page 70).

Over time, freight and passenger railroad service into the hotsprings community of Calistoga (Napa County) was supplanted by trucks and buses. Calistoga lost both its SP Branch (formerly the Napa Valley Railroad) and the San Francisco, Napa & Calistoga interurban. A railroad that sticks with only a single industry and cannot diversify stands a good chance of perishing.

Here are some sketches of a few of those railroads that have passed into memory.

Death Valley Railroad, Ryan-- Death Valley, Inyo County

Up on the sides of Pyramid Peak in Death Valley National Monument, several long low buildings sit incongruously, like shelves on a barren rock pile. These buildings are collectively called "Ryan," and they house some of the miners who work the nearby digs of the U.S. Borax Company. I visited the desolate, unfriendly town of Ryan on a day when the temperature was 118 degrees. I did not exactly feel welcome: For reasons that were never explained, I was not permitted to take photos; there was no water for fifteen miles, and the pistons of my automobile motor froze up, so to speak.

In this forlorn place, the Pacific Borax Company constructed the three-foot-gauge Death Valley RR in 1914 to carry its ores to Death Valley Junction and the Tonopah & Tidewater RR (see p. 19). By 1926, richer deposits were encountered near Boron, California, and mining in Ryan was halted. In 1931, the DVRR died.

The mine road itself, a two-foot-wide, gasoline-powered line called the "Baby Gauge," was pressed into tourist service along the precarious overlooks and through dark tunnels. The Baby Gauge remained in operation until 1950.

Today, the exceptionally well-constructed, twenty-mile roadbed (still owned by U.S. Borax) shows its masonry shorings; locomotive #2 a fine Baldwin 2-8-0 (1916) rests in the nearby Furnace Creek Museum, along with a tiny Baby Gauge engine; and the DVRR's 1928 #5 Brill passenger car decays on a track at the Laws Railroad Museum near Bishop. One Baby Gauge engine is still in operation, far from prying public eyes, at a portion of the intermittently open Ryan mine.

Mill Valley & Mt. Tamalpais Scenic Railway, Marin County

This picture of an outing on the Mt. Tamalpais line passing though Muir Woods was taken in 1917.

It was in January of 1896 when a group of sharp-eyed Mill Valley businessmen eyed the top of Mt. Tamalpais, the "Fujiyama" of San Francisco Bay, as a likely place for a railroad terminal.

On February 5th, construction began; on March 4th, an engine arrived; on March 7th, teamsters struck (presumably they were pacified the next day); and by March 17th, rails started being laid. On March 18th, irate citizens, whose driveways and trees were being chewed up, obtained an injunction; over the next six days, ties and rails were laid out anyway; and on March 23rd, a cooperative judge withdrew the injunction. Although a few newspapers griped about management irregularities, the construction proceeded. On August 18th, the last spike was driven, and on August 22nd, the first train went up. This speedy little drama illustrates the fine art of "railroading" — a complete railroad was built in only months.

In 1907, Muir Woods was blessed with a branch line to what is now Camp Eastwood. Few people complained about the slashing of the mountainside and the redwoods, for in that era of slapdash construction, the line was built with some care. Afterwards, it was praised by all the right people, from Teddy Roosevelt to Robert Louis Stevenson, as well as by contemporary travel guides.

For thirty-four years, this spectacular road carried hundreds of thousands of passengers to the very summit of Mt. Tam, as well as to the depths of that great redwood forest below, Muir Woods. Still, at a time when trackworker's worth was about $2 a day, the $1.50 that it cost to the top made the MV&MTRR a comparative luxury.

Trains going down this road — whose continuous downslope had a mere 5-percent grade — had to navigate an astronomical 281 curves. Thus the MV&MTRR became known as "The Crookedest Railroad in the World."

(Some pains were taken to disclaim any relation between this title and the epithet often attributed to the Southern Pacific.)

Safety features, which surfaced only occasionally on other contemporary railroads, were so effective here that no passenger lives were ever lost. The only recorded fatality occurred when an out-of-control engine overturned on tracks that had, in an overzealous attempt to cut down wheel squeals on sharp curves, been greased. (For some streetcars, San Francisco's Muni still greases its tracks — but only on level stretches.)

The MV&MTRR's cars were mostly of an "excursion" type (flatcars with a canopy) or smaller "gravity cars." These "gravities" were pulled to the top of the grade in trains, then released singly, with only a brakeman in control. Imagine the immense pleasure of gliding silently, for forty-five minutes, down the mountainside at ten m.p.h. through some of the most lovely scenery in California.

This railroad died in 1930, a casualty brought about by the emergence of cars and hard times.

Remnants:

Engine #9, two-truck Heisler (1920) — now on display at the Pacific Lumber Company Museum in Scotia.

Gravity car, wheelless — awaiting restoration at the Castro Point Railway yards, Richmond.

Mill Valley (bus) terminal — served both the MV&MTRR and NWP branch line from Sausalito.

Stonework foundation at the summit of Mt. Tamalpais. Formerly the site of a fine inn and the upper terminal, this now ignominiously underlies a restroom.

Perfect roadbed from E. Blithedale Rd. to summit, and Camp Eastwood (Muir Woods) to junction above Mountain Home — now a hiking and biking path.

The North Pacific Coast (Narrow Gauge) Railroad, Sausalito, Marin County--Cazadero, Sonoma County

Communities become fond of their railroads. Even the engines become part of the family. And like many a family member, they are most appreciated when they are gone.

Along the Marin coast north of San Francisco, the roads are narrow and winding, subject to slides, and often foggy. Back in 1870, transport was offered only by rough wagons that clattered over precipitous mud roads, or by light coastal boats. And since both were at the mercy of the wind and the rain, a narrow-gauge railroad was touted as the solution to connect the Tomales Bay communities with San Francisco Bay's Sausalito. Thus, in June of 1874, the North Pacific Coast Railroad was born.

The NPC's opening days were roses — all the way to the coastal fishing town of Tomales, and later to the tiny dairying town of Cazadero. But the usual set of catastrophes occurred — derailing, washouts, the sinking of its ferryboat — and then the NPC's honeymoon was over. For years, the little line struggled to keep its trains on the tracks and, since it was in part a commuter line to San Francisco, its ferryboats above water.

During the years of its existence, the NPC (renamed the North Shore Railroad in 1902) was the Bay Area's favorite excursion road; but since this kind of activity just didn't pay, it was finally bought out by the SP — who, true to form, closed it in 1933. As last rites, the community gave the Marin Coast's fifty-nine-year-old family member a funeral procession and a picnic-wake.

Remnants:

Engine #12, 4-4-0 Baldwin (1876), property of the Railway and Locomotive Historical Society.

The "Electra" (standard gauge) electric interurban, as Pacific Electric's #1544 at Travel Town, Los Angeles.

Railroad shed, now a community center, in Point Reyes Station.

Roadbed along Tomales Bay.

Partial Northwestern Pacific roadbed, Sausalito-Mill Valley.

No. 13 of the North Pacific Coast awaits refueling at Sausalito.

Pacific Coast (Narrow Gauge) Railway, Avila, San Luis Obispo County-- Los Olivos, Santa Barbara County

In a windy, hilly, duney part of the Pacific coast in San Luis Obispo County in 1875, a group of local citizens began to think of a narrow-gauge railroad as the solution to their transportation woes. The coastal town of Avila and the inland communities of San Luis Obispo and Central City (Santa Maria) needed a convenient way of getting around the coast's round, bare hills. Only one year later, in the summer of 1876, Central City saw its first train of the new Pacific Coast Railway.

The fertile Santa Maria Valley was fast becoming an agricultural center, specializing in grain and seed. To make the most of the valley's production, the PCR extended its tracks, through rugged coastal hills, to its terminus in Los Olivos.

An odd circumstance that helped the early PCR survive was the 1877 completion of the SP coast route north to Santa Barbara and south to Lompoc — and no further. Logically, the SP's proximity might smother the dwarfish PCR; but miraculously, the SP stopped building, leaving a fifty-mile gap. In order to make a through trip, most travelers from San Francisco to Los Angeles chose to change to the PCR in San Luis Obispo and then board the stage to Santa Barbara from Los Olivos, frequently dining at the fine Mattei's Tavern, which stands there to this day.

The SP did bridge its gap in 1901, but by then the PCR was so well established that it managed to parallel the giant for another thirty-two years. Finally, in 1933, the PCR gave way to Model-Ts, Model-As, and the Depression; and the last, tearful ride was made.

Remnants:

Mattei's Tavern, Los Olivos, founded 1886 — a resort for Hollywooders long after the PCR folded.

Roadbed alongside Hwy. 154 near its junction with Hwy. 101.

Roadbed (now standard gauge) — partly used by Santa Maria Valley RR for local freight, in western Santa Maria, at the crossroads of the two lines.

The Sonoma Valley Prismoidal Railway, Sonoma County, and The Epsom Salts Railroad, San Bernardino County-- Early Monorails

The Disneyland Monorail wasn't California's first. Neither were the Los Angeles County Fairgound or the Cal Expo Monorail. The original monorail was built back in 1876, three miles of a contraption called the Sonoma Valley Prismoidal Railway. It was the beginning of a port-to-town transport system for Sonoma, seat of the northernmost of the California missions.

This novel machine, consisting of a triangular mound of earth, was planked over on the sides and topped by a single rail. The steam engine and its cars ran on the single rail; ancillary wheels on either side kept the balance. Apparently, this system worked well enough — but lacking the resources to build bridges, when no easy way of getting wagons across the ''track'' was found, the money ran out. Two years later, the right-of-way was converted into what later became a branch of the Northwestern Pacific Railroad.

To soothe Americans' aching feet, another monorail was built in 1923 to carry Epsom salts to Searles Lake from a Panamint Mountain mine. This one had the same general shape as the SVPR, but A-frame trestles were used instead of a mound of earth. The engines used tractor motors and, like the cars, ran on double-flanged wheels, with bracing wheels on the sides. The twenty-eight-mile Epsom Salts Railroad ran for a remarkable three years, on grades as steep as 12 percent. But the mine played out; and the rain, in that desert region, caused several trestle washouts and occasionally softened the Searles Lake bed on which the trestle was partly laid. The Epsom Salts' last train ran in 1926, unmourned.

Yosemite Valley Railroad, Merced, Merced County-- El Portal, Mariposa County

Yosemite Park was created by Congress in 1890, and it didn't take long for a clamor to arise: "The Park must be made more accessible to the visitor." This cry is still heard today. But in those pre-auto days, railroads were the only way to bring the visitors in.

It took considerable effort and $10 million, but on May 15, 1907, all seventy-eight miles of the Yosemite Valley Railroad, which stretched from Merced to El Portal along the Merced River Valley, opened for service. It was immediately patronized by kings and commoners, presidents and proletariat. And the incoming lumbering industry encouraged the YV's business as a passenger line.

The Yosemite Lumber Company installed impressive, inclined cable-railways that fed directly into the YV line. The railroad closed for four years during the Depression; reopened; sold its logged-out land to the Forest Service in 1944; and finally folded. Another industry along the line, the Yosemite Portland Cement Company, closed the same year.

Once again, the auto took its toll, and in 1945, its final year, the YV carried only 584 passengers. When it died, it was mourned — but without fanfare.

Remnants:

A dusty National Park Service pioneer transport museum in El Portal has an old station and Engine #6, three-truck Shay (1927), ex-Hetch-Hetchy RR, which was first used in construction of the dam, and later by the Pickering Lumber Company.

A long, hikeable roadbed, Merced Falls to El Portal.

These are the unfortunate stories of a few lines that didn't make it, victims of the Depression and America's love affair with the internal combustion engine. They passed away at a time when people were tired of steam railroads and wanted something new and different. Now, forty-five years later, a steam railroad is viewed as something special and rare; and as we shall see, the development of the diesel engine spawned the rebirth of railroading.

A surprising number of short lines still survive, however. But survival takes many forms. Some are nothing more than tracks and a station or two, operated by one or more of the big lines; others operate independently, with several big-line owners; and still others maintain complete owner-operator independence. Later in this book, we'll take a look at these lines and see how they survive.

But first, let's look at the rise and near-extinction of rails in public transit.

Expansion and Eventual Decline of Public Transit (1880s-1920s)

While the major and short-line railroads were available to transport the public from town to city, rails within the towns grew only very slowly. Horse cars started their clopping rounds early in San Francisco — 1857 — but most towns didn't lay their rails until the 1880s.

Not long after this, electricity indirectly helped clean up the streets: local power companies were able to give more reliable service for cable and trolley motors than the horse-powered vehicles could and so, fewer horses.

Cable cars began tugging up San Francisco streets in 1873. In 1885, this clanking new idea spread to Los Angeles; but the recession of 1893 forced all but the most hardy to close.

Most towns' local trolley lines expanded along with their populations — until, in the 1920s, the motorcar clogged their streets and the populace turned away from public transit. Nevertheless, San Francisco and Los Angeles continued to expand their lines, especially their interurban service. San Francisco added its last streetcar line in 1928, but didn't consolidate all its municipal lines until 1944, when the city took over full operation.

The entire Los Angeles basin was especially fortunate in having its immense distances unified under a single (although private) sponsorship as early as 1908. In that year, some existing Southern Pacific interurban lines combined with the already vast Pacific Electric Railway Company, which had been founded in 1901 by Collis Huntington's nephew, Henry. This new line, which used a huge interlocking system that peaked around 1926, controlled nearly all local and interurban transit in four counties.

This was the era of the "Big Red Cars." These ran on approximately twenty interurban lines, blanketing the area on 1,600 miles of track from Riverside to Santa Monica and from San Fernando to Redlands. In Los Angeles alone, there were fifty-eight streetcar lines — the "Yellow Cars." It was the nation's vastest and fastest transit system. Running time from downtown Los Angeles was given at sixty minutes to Covina and fifty-seven minutes to Redondo Beach. Try that now at rush hour!

But before long, strains of the same old mournful song began to be heard. Since commuters had fewer jobs to go to in 1933, ridership dropped, and so did service. In 1953, the once-proud PE was sold to the Metropolitan Coach Lines, whose very name foretold the fate of the electric railroads. The last Los Angeles streetcar ran in 1963. Years later, in 1976, a governmental committee uncovered what the contemporary public, helplessly watching the electric service decline, had always suspected — bus manufacturers, as early as the 1930s, had made secret pacts to sell their wares if the electrics were displaced.

Just as San Francisco is known for its cable cars, Los Angeles once was known for its funiculars. One of these was Angel's Flight, a railway exactly 0.076 miles in length that was built in 1901 to scale Los Angeles' Bunker Hill. Interest in this marvel rose but then waned; and with the death of public interest, so died the Angel's Flight. All that remains now is a concrete foundation — although a corps of railfans, pushing to have it restored, may do just that very soon, using pieces of that funicular (currently in storage).

PE's probably most fascinating line was Pasadena's Mt. Lowe Railway — a 50-percent grade incline railway, two-thirds of a mile long, that connected to a winding electric line at its upper terminus. These two sets of tracks formed a magnificent unique railroad attraction that lasted from 1893 to 1938.

Since there's not much left of all those electric transit systems now, it's refreshing to see San Francisco refurbishing its five remaining streetcar lines and equipment (see p. 66). The famous BART (Bay Area Rapid Transit) (see p. 67) is a meager "replacement" for the former network of the Key System and Interurban Electric Transit of the East (San Francisco) Bay.

Currently, the California Railway Museum (see p. 89) and the Orange Empire Railway Museum (see p. 131) offer some nostalgic rides on well-kept equipment. Other locations, such as Los Angeles' Travel Town (see p. 140) and Fairgrounds, display a few pieces that were rescued from the scrap heap. Los Angeles has many of those old rights-of-way, still with their unused tracks in place. Will they ever be the nuclei for a new really rapid transit system?

Sic transit transit.

Taking a trip on a passenger train was a popular adventure around the turn of the century.

A Sampling of Former Electric Transit in California

Local Street Trolley Lines	Remarks
Bakersfield	Began 1900.
East (San Francisco) Bay	Large network, Berkeley-Oakland area.
Eureka	12½ miles in 1913.
Fresno	
Los Angeles	1889 (horse); electric to 1963.
Monterey-Pacific Grove	1891 (horse), electric until 1923.
Ontario	Began 1883.
Riverside	
Sacramento	Began 1890.
San Bernardino	
San Diego-National City	1886 (horse); 1887 electric.
San Francisco	1857-1913 (horse); 1891 (electric —several companies) to present (Muni).
San Jose	1868 (horse); 1877 (People's Horse RR Company).
Santa Barbara	
Santa Cruz	
Santa Rosa	
Stockton	

An Oakland, Antioch, & Eastern interurban awaiting its next call to service in the East Bay.

Interurbans

Alameda-Contra Costa Counties	Key System, Interurban Electric Ry., Sacramento Northern.
Central Valley Counties — Butte, Sacramento, San Joaquin, Solano, Sutter	Central California Traction, Sacramento Northern.
Imperial County	Holtville Interurban.
Los Angeles County	1895, as Pacific Electric expanded over region until 1961.
Marin County	1903-1941 (North Shore RR).
Napa County	Napa Valley Electric.
Nevada County	1902-1924 (Nevada County Traction).
Orange County	PE.
Riverside County	PE (initially four lines).
San Francisco County	1906-1920 (Ocean Shore electric to company line).
San Mateo County	1906-1920 (Interurban; Ocean Shore steam).
Santa Barbara County	Santa Maria-Guadalupe.
Santa Clara County	Peninsular Ry.
Sonoma County	1878-1890 (Sonoma Valley RR — narrow gauge, 1878-1890; standard, 1890); 1887 (Santa Rosa & Carquinez RR); 1904-1932 (Petaluma & Santa Rosa).
Stanislaus County	Modesto & Empire Traction.

Note: This listing isn't meant to be exhaustive, only to indicate how very many areas once were served by electric railroad systems.

Early California Cable Car Systems

City and Company	Remarks	Maximum Percent of Grade
Oakland		
Oakland Cable Ry.	1886-1893 (electric 1899)	flat
Consolidated Piedmont Cable Company	1890 (electric 1896)	14.5
San Diego		
San Diego Cable Ry.	1890-1892 (electric 1896)	8
Los Angeles		
Second Street Cable Ry.	1885-1889	27.7
Temple Street Cable Ry.	1886-1902 (electric, 1902-1946)	flat
Pacific Ry.	1889-1896 (electric 1896)	flat
San Francisco		
Clay Street Hill Company	1873-1891	17
Sutter Street Ry.	1877-1906 (electric 1929; 5-foot gauge)	
California Street Cable RR	1878-present	18.2
Geary Street Park & Ocean RR	1880-1912 (5', then standard, 1902)	11.4
Presidio & Ferries RR	1880-1906 (5')	
Market Street Cable Ry.	1883-1941 (standard gauge)	18.4
Ferries & Cliff House RR	1888-present (later United Rys., Muni)	18.7
Omnibus RR & Cable Company	1889-1899 (present Muni barn)	10.9

Note: 42″ gauge unless othewise noted. Most lines were about three to four miles long.

An historic meet of the ''Genoa''
(''Jupiter''), Western Pacific's Old 94 and
W.P.'s ''California Zephyr'' on the
Feather River Route, near Quincy.

The Depression and the Internal Combustion Engine (1930s)

The history of California's railroads has abounded with sad tales of the "little trains that couldn't" — because of a logged-out forest, a played-out mine, or an overreaching or unimaginative management. But beyond these details, other, larger external events moved many roads to their ultimate extinction.

An operating railroad has never been and can never be a lasting thing if it is supported by charity alone. In order to be workable, it must be profitable. This is most important in terms of the short line, whose existence is always the most precarious. And as much as we may decry occasional corporate insensitivity, corporations have been the strength of lines like the Southern Pacific.

Although the great financial recessions and "panics" of the last hundred years were hard on the long-haul roads, they did survive — their continued existence was not so much threatened as altered. But not so the short lines — as we have seen in the cases of the ephemeral YV, the MV&MT, the PCR, and the NPC, all of which closed between 1930 and 1933.

Much or all of their traffic depended on passenger movement; and during the Depression era, the public simply couldn't afford to travel. With money in short supply, the demand for freight declined calamitously.

The written histories of most railroads don't reveal the good they do; instead, they are histories of disasters — floods, wrecks, landslides, earthquakes, recession, and strikes.

To a short line, any slight reverse, such as any one of the above, constituted a major disaster; and, confronted with such misfortunes, the short lines failed. A 1926 Railroad Commission map listed nearly forty independent railroad companies operating in California. In 1975, the figure was twenty-six. Today, in 1978, there are fewer than eighteen truly independent lines, not counting several exclusively excursion lines and dozens of U.S. Government military lines.

Here and there in this book, I have referred to the other big railroad menace — the gasoline engine. Let a few statistics tell the story. In 1929, the doomed Yosemite Valley RR carried 25,912 passengers; in 1944, its last year, it carried only 584. As early as 1917, more people traveled to Yosemite Park by auto than by train. The Mt. Tam RR, strictly a passenger road, earned a profit of $19,584 in 1923; by 1924, the profit was down to $6,032 — the new auto road had done its job.

In 1945, a congressional committee reported that the U.S. Government had already supplied U.S. railroads with land worth $126 million, through the Land Grant Act. By 1970, the government's annual budget for roads and highways had grown to $4.6 billion!

A similar tale may be told of the trucking industry's ability to handle smaller freight over those costly highways, and another of the relative ease of bus and plane travel — but we already know these tales. Most railroads in the '30s were letting their passenger service slip because they saw their survival in the freight-hauling business.

Some railroads, like the WP and the Santa Fe, kept their passenger orientation; but most simply knuckled under to the proponents of the airplane and the internal combustion engine.

The time was ripe for the auto and the airplane to receive the public's largesse in the form of highways and airport subsidies. The love affair with the train was over. The age of speedier speed was beginning to accelerate.

The Diesel and the Airplane (1940s-1950s)

Steam engines as a major motive power disappeared in the mid-'50s, when diesel (and occasional electric) power was adopted almost universally. And as the power up front changed, so did the cars behind.

By 1960, because of the prodigious postwar production of autos and jet planes, long-distance railroad passenger service almost disppeared. And as the public used these new vehicles to get where they were going, its familiarity with railroads diminshed. People began to view the train, both steam and diesel, as merely a noisy, ugly thing that sometimes kept them impatiently waiting at a railroad crossing. The romance, safety, and relative leisureliness of train travel no longer appealed to them.

The diesel engine may not be as romantic as the steam locomotive, but it certainly is more efficient; and seen at the head of Amtrak's quicksilver caterpillars, it is almost as awe-inspiring. These new shiny diesels seem glamorous to a public accustomed to the old clangorous, smoky steamers. Frequently, when I was a child, my father dressed me in my pajamas and drove me, in the nighttime darkness, to watch and hear the Seaboard Airline Railway's brand new "Silver Meteor" hum into town at 9 P.M.

Recently, in Stockton, I was treated to a cab ride in a 1933 Electro Motive Corporation diesel — as rattly as a dice cup in a San Francisco bar, and spouting more smoke and sparks than the 1976 Freedom Train steamer (originally, SP's #4449). Sure, it was exciting, as any rail ride is.

Following World War II, the application of diesel motive power by the railroads was swift, especially on the western roads, where the new diesels could make their long runs without the necessity for frequent fuel and water stops. The War had proven the efficacy of the diesel. Many easily-managed local switch engines were acquired from the Army or Navy, which had found them indispensable for yard work.

Stewart Holbrook, in his "Story of American Railroads" rather underestimated in 1947 the rapid demise of the steam locomotive. He assumed steam would be around for at least twenty years. But as of this writing, I know of only four California common carriers that still carry steam on their rosters, and only two of those operate regularly.

The diesel is simply a more efficient machine. It requires little water, it starts rapidly, it furnishes power instantly, it burns a fuel which, until recently, has been relatively cheap. (It is almost ironic that the California Western now keeps its oil-burning steamers off the steep slopes, since they fairly guzzle that now-costly fluid. Maybe they should go back to wood?)

During the 1940s, for those to whom rail travel still was *the* means of choice, a few railroads maintained, and often considerably improved their equipment and service — using the more reliable, speedier, and cleaner diesel. The first diesel streamliner appeared in California in 1936, as SP's "City of San Francisco;" the Santa Fe began the first long-haul diesel freight in 1941. In California, this heavier type of engine was incorporated into regular, long-haul passenger service in the '30s and '40s, with the inauguration of WP's "Zephyrs," the SP's "Sunset Limiteds'" and the Santa Fe's "Superchiefs" — all very special trains, some of whose names survive today in Amtrak schedules.

But since the airlines, quick to capitalize on their superior long-haul speed, began attracting passengers, the railroad companies slowly relinquished the field. Often, the public was disgusted and dismayed — but it also was fickle, riding in cars and planes in droves, though frequently only in response to the railroad cutbacks.

Inevitably, the diesels multiplied and, needing far less attention than their predecessors, took over the profitable and burgeoning, heavy-freight traffic. By the middle 1950s, few steamers had escaped the scrap heap. Those that did were religiously cared for by nostalgic steamfans, eager to preserve the history of the railroads.

Subsequent to Steam (1950s-Present)

Despite the challenge from autos, planes, and trucks, the development of powerful and swift diesel equipment eventually planted the notion of rapid and efficient service, both passenger and freight, in the often lethargic minds of railroad directorates. With new equipment and computerization techniques (partly borrowed from the airlines), railroads once again began to grow in importance and stature in the public eye.

The last twenty years has seen a revolution in the freight-handling system of California's railroads, and a massive effort to return to the most pleasurable, efficient, and pollution-free aspects of rapid streamliner passenger service.

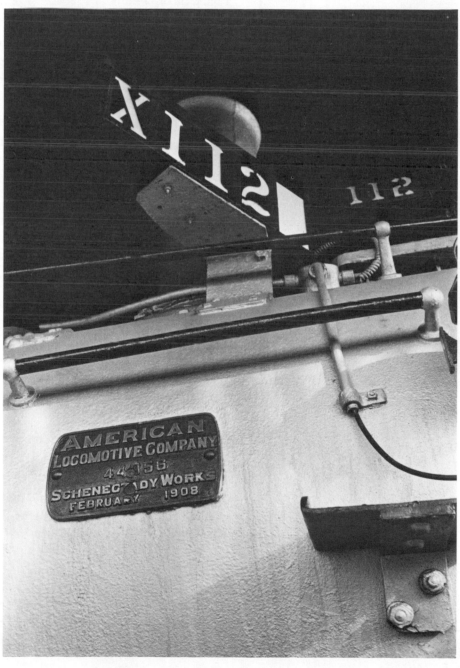

Passengers: Amtrak and SP (1970s)

The National Railroad Passenger Corporation (as Amtrak is officially known), formed in 1971, took upon itself the task of revitalizing the rail passenger service of America. California, with its more than thirty-five stations, was the recipient of much of this service.

Because it is a governmental agency, Amtrak has its budget problems. It has been accused of being a deep money-sink; but its ridership has increased steadily, keeping literally thousands of buses and cars off the highways. Recently, some of this public money has gone into the purchase of the old Santa Fe Ninth Street coach repair yards and the adjacent Redondo engine repair shops in Los Angeles. These two purchases will immediately lower Amtrak repair costs that formerly had to be spent on outside contractors.

However, political gremlins are at work. As the "San Joaquin" (Oakland-Bakersfield) ridership has increased to near capacity on the train's daily runs, some legislators, who neither understand nor care for rail travel, have attempted to cut two days' service.

Amtrak's service, like its finances, has also drawn criticism. The same old bugaboos — like weather-undermined track, derailments, and malfunctioning cars — continue to plague its lines. On a twelve-hour intrastate run, there have been delays of up to an hour. But since that would hardly be serious for an airline, is it fair to expect that much more from a railroad?

I hear some complaints about the food on Amtrak. Probably they are justified. But I hear few complaints about the generally cheerful staff and personal service aboard. And I see a new generation — *thousands* of young people — riding their first train; and thousands more their second.

As for the roadbed, Amtrak rides upon the rails of the SP and the Santa Fe, and the "rent" paid to these lines for track upkeep is considerable. Let the riders who feel aggrieved by such roadbed problems direct their complaints to the road, where the fault may lie.

The SP alone remains in the California commuting business, although it keeps using its old tricks to try to weasel out. It received bad marks from a 1968 ICC report, which said, "The record is convincing that the SP has deliberately set out to discourage existing, as well as new, patronage. . . ." Nevertheless, it must be said that its remaining service between San Francisco and San Jose is commendably frequent, on time, speedy, and comfortable. The fare on this stretch of track is only about $3.00. In 1863, the fare was $2.50, which must mean a lot of increased efficiency and ridership to keep the fare down.

The SP claims a "loss" on this line. But if you read their figures carefully, you'd see that there is no loss — they simply are not making *as much* as they would if they abandoned their passenger service.

Beautiful old passenger stations, like this one in Burlingame, have become Historic Landmarks.

Freight: The Modern Railroad (1970s)

This is one of Southern Pacific's new freight locomotives hauling a unit train.

As recently as 1971, a former special assistant to the secretary of transportation gloomily wrote that the railroads were in trouble.[1] Soon after, the New York Central and the Pennsylvania Railroad folded into government ownership (as Conrail). But in California, the scene was different.

In August 1977, Milt Moskowitz reported in the San Francisco *Chronicle* that the five largest profit makers in U.S. transportation were railroads, and that three of those were in California (UP, AT&SF, and SP). It appears that somebody at the top has finally been getting it all together.

What do we see when we look around? Unit trains, in which all the cars carry identical cargoes, point to point; swift piggyback truck-rail trains, combining the best of truck, rail, and ship door-to-door service that really is *service;* and new, huge, specialized freight cars.

All these complex systems are controlled by a centralized computer. At 2 A.M. one morning, I appeared at SP's Mojave dispatcher's office and was offered a demonstration. I gave the computer operator the number of a specific locomotive, he fingered a few buttons and in seconds, the readout reported that the loco was in use and just out of Ogden, heading west.

The huge sorting yards, like the Santa Fe's humpyard in Barstow, are all computerized, as well. In seconds, electronic sensors pick up the cars' numbers (which are printed in multicolored code on every piece of equipment), weigh the cars, check their destinations, indicate the proper switch track, and then print out the list of cars on each track. The railroads have finally gone modern.

Many of the remaining short lines are flourishing because of their increased and diversified trade. Rate schedules and good management are enabling these lines to have a continued, profitable existence. Lately, a few have been absorbed by or come under control of the larger lines. And another few are just holding on. But today, very few tracks have seen all operations cease, as they did in the 1930s and '40s. Shippers are finding the rejuvenated rail systems their real method of choice.

It's exciting to be around railroads in a new era. This guide, then is your opportunity to go look, to ride, and to experience for yourself the excitement of both old and new trains and equipment.

All aboard!

---

[1] John Burby, *The Great American Motion Sickness or Why You Can't Get There From Here* (Boston: Little, Brown & Co., 1971).

Railfan Shoptalk

Engine Classification

When you see an engine, there's a very easy way to classify it. For instance, let's try California Western's engine #45. In this guide, you'll see that it is called a 2-8-2 Baldwin Mikado (1924), affectionately called a "Mike."

The wheel arrangement numbering is first and goes like this: small front (guide) wheels — large driving wheels — small rear trailing wheels (under the cab). If there are no small wheels, we use "0," as in an 0-4-0 switcher or 0-4-0 diesel. If there is no tender and the water tank is on the engine, we simply add "T" for "tank," as in 2-6-2T.

Several engines are designated "Shay" or "Heisler," after their designers. These engines have no guide wheels, and *all* the wheels are driven by a powerful bevel gear arrangement in sets of four, called "trucks." Other gear-driven lomotives in this book are "Dolbeer" (a logging engine) (p. 60) and "Climax" (a Shay-like engine) (pp. 92 and 139).

Next we give the builder of the engine (and sometimes the shop), followed by the commonly used name of the wheel arrangement (if there is one). For example, a 4-4-2 engine is called an "Atlantic," and a 4-6-2 is called a "Pacific."

Finally comes the year the engine was built (in parentheses).

Diesels are usually classified here by their builder, the tonnage, and the year built. Other terms used are "switcher," for yard use, and "road engine," for the long hauls.

Couplings

The *link and pin* is the earliest and simplest type of coupling, and consists of nothing more than a drawbar that fits into a slot, and a pin that holds it there. This type is used on streetcars, cable cars, and some old steam trains. Careless use of this manual coupler has resulted in the loss of many hands.

The *knuckle coupler* is an automatic coupling device, like two hands clasped, invented in the 1880s. It is the standard coupler used on all U.S. railroads since 1893, thanks to the efforts of one Lorenzo Coffin (1823-1915).

In Antelope, changing a wheel on a boxcar is not the same as changing the tire on a car — it is actually easier.

Rolling Stock or Passenger and Freight Cars

Most of these types are evident from their names, like boxcar, tankcar, flatcar (flat), or coach. A *gondola* is a flatcar with sides, and can carry passengers or freight. A *hopper* car has chutes in the bottom and carries loose material such as coal or gravel. A refrigerator car is often called a *reefer*, as in the trucking industry. The word *caboose* may come from the Spanish "cabo" (head), where the head man, or conductor, rides.

An *observation* car is a passenger car with an open platform on the end (the spot where presidential candidates like to speak). A *Pullman* is a sleeping car, first built by the Pullman Company.

And a *tender,* just behind the engine on most steamers, tends to the engine's needs with fuel and water. A *combo* is a combination baggage and passenger car. The term *M/W* is maintenance-of-way, and *R/W* is the right-of-way.

Taking in the view from the observation car during an excursion in the 1930s.

Gauges

We find three gauges, or rail widths, in common use around the state. The *narrow* gauge used by the cable cars is three feet, six inches. A narrow gauge enables the car to turn sharp corners, perfect for narrow city streets. BART uses a *broad* gauge at five feet, six inches. This gauge gives exceptional stability on turns at very high speeds, perfect for BART's high-speed trains that must twist around many obstacles. *Standard* gauge, a compromise between these, is used by all U.S. railroads and (with modified turning radius) by San Francisco streetcars; it is four feet, eight and a half inches, with only one-eighth-inch tolerance.

Some of the ''short line'' railroads in the state use other narrow gauges, but they are uncommon.

The narrowest passenger-carrying gauge around is two and a half inches — a model road mounted on trestles so that the engineer straddles his real steam engine. They're to be found at the Live Steamers clubs in Berkeley, Los Angeles, and Chula Vista.

The widest passenger-carrying devices have a ninety-foot gauge! They're the electrically driven painters' trolleys beneath the Golden Gate Bridge, suspended from rails along the outer edges of the highway structure. The longest goes about one mile, hanging precariously, 700 feet above the swirling water.

Another type of extra-wide rails in the state that carry an operator is the crane gantry, to be found at several port facilities in the harbor areas.

PART II
CALIFORNIA RAILROADS TODAY

California North of San Francisco Bay-Sacramento Area

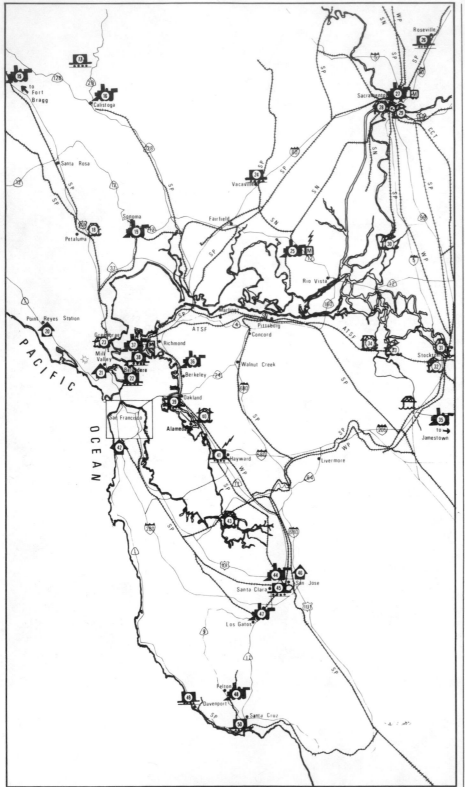

The California mountains of the Coast Range, and the Sierras northward from the thirty-ninth parallel to the Cascades, offer an element that gives railroading a distinctive character — trees — and, consequently, lumbering.

Here, now as in years past, trees grow faster than anywhere else in the state. In winter, almost daily, it rains in the west and snows in the east. With the trees come the lumberjacks; years before, the spidery network of narrow-gauge rails came with them. Now there are no such rails left, since huge diesel machines can handle the timber more efficiently; but the lumbering still goes on, and it's still the railroads that do most of the work of hauling the lumber to market.

15	California Western RR
16	Calistoga Steam RR
17	Old mercury mine
18	Swingbridge
19	Sonoma Gaslight and Western RR
20	Old station North Pacific Coast RR
21	Old terminal NW'n Pacific and Mt Tamalpais RR
22	Old NW'n Pacific docks
23	Drawbridge
24	Nut Tree RR
25	California Rwy. Museum
26	Southern Pacific shops
27	Central Pacific Station
28	Swingbridge
29	Drawbridge
30	Drawbridge
31	Swingbridge
32	Drawbridge
33	Drawbridge
34	Swingbridge
35	Sierra RR
36	Redwood Valley RR
37	Castro Point RR
38	Richmond Mole
39	Oakland Terminal Rwy
40	Alameda Belt lift bridge
41	BART shops
42	Old Station Ocean Shore RR
43	Swingbridges Salt pan RR
44	Great America Park
45	Southern Pacific roundhouse
46	Amtrak-SP depot
47	Billy Jones Wildcat RR
48	Roaring Camp and Big Trees RR
49	Remnant of Ocean Shore RR
50	Roller Coaster

Rail Rides, Standard and Narrow Gauges

Alton & Pacific Railroad, Alton Humboldt County

Back in 1884, inhabitants of the Eel River Valley needed a railroad to get around, so the Eel River & Eureka Railroad, from Eureka to Hydesville, was built. Today, that route is the Carlotta branch of the NWP (SP), but alongside the right-of-way at Alton is a most unusual rail ride, created by a dedicated railfan named Frank Bayliss.

Bayliss managed to find a wood-burning, two-foot-gauge German steam engine, which he uses to pull a unique mixed train around his acreage. He also has a collection of very interesting railroad antiques.

His yard, illustrative of Bayliss's prodigious one-man activity, is a bit cluttered, and the prolific brambles hide some of the larger pieces. But the ride is quite a thrill, and Bayliss also has a lot of double-gauge track, some shops, and even a turntable.

Frank Bayliss (A&PRR), Rte. 1, Box 477, Alton, CA 95540, *no phone.*

Equipment: 24″ and standard gauges, one and a half-mile ride.

Locos (2′), **live:** #5, 0-4-0 Orenstein & Koppel (1935); 0-4-0 Plymouth switcher; in restoration, #1, 0-6-0 John Fowler (c. 1900), ex-Fiji Island cane fields. (standard gauge): #M62, two-truck Heisler converted to Murphy diesel in the late 1930s; Napa Valley & Calistoga interurban #63; NV&C box motor #100.

Rolling stock: (2′): Two passenger cars, two passenger gondolas, one caboose.

On display: NWP chair car.

Schedule: Memorial-Labor Day, Thurs.-Tues. (closed Wed.).

Fare: $1.50.

Also: Picnic facilities.

Amtrak (North)

North of the San Francisco Bay area, Amtrak stops in three California towns — Orland, Redding, and Dunsmuir — and in nearby Klamath Falls, Oregon. It's probably the easiest ride in Northern California, but only a few people will want to ride just this short distance — the schedules, unfortunately, run around midnight to 3 A.M.!

California Western Railroad, Ft. Bragg-Willits, Mendocino County

In 1885, the logging and fishing town of Ft. Bragg in Northern California had a lumber company, plenty of trees, and a port of sorts, but no good roads through the thick redwoods or along the rough coastline. To get those trees to the port and the Ft. Bragg Lumber Company, the Ft. Bragg Railroad was founded — with some hope that, sooner or later, it might join the growing network of California railroads.

It was later — as a matter of fact, some twenty-seven years later — before passenger service was instituted from the Northwestern Pacific's division town of Willits, only forty miles east. During that time, the engines of the railroad were busy hauling their trains down to the sea and ships.

Meanwhile, the Ft. Bragg Lumber Company became the Union Lumber Company, and the Fort Bragg RR became the California Western. Once it had connected with the NWP, the CW flourished — not only as a lumber road, but also as a fine excursion route through the redwoods, and as an immigrant route from the east to the coast.

The grand terrain of the CW makes it a rather expensive road to maintain. There are thirty-one trestles and bridges. Washouts and landslides are common. The 3.3-percent grade is very steep for locomotives — so much that at present, the steam locos used on the line stick to only the lower elevations, letting the diesels complete the run to Willits from Northspur, instead.

A "Super Skunk" of the California Western Railroad, one of the few standard-gauge steam railroads operating on a regular schedule on the West Coast.

As with all other passenger-carrying railroads, the number of passengers fell off considerably in the '20s and '30s. The Cal Western met the challenge as did few other railroads of the era. Instead of bearing the great expense of huge steamers pulling half-empty coaches, it instituted the gasoline railbus. To a population used to sniffing wood and coal smoke, the gasoline fumes were not particularly fragrant, and the rail lines were soon blessed with a pet name, the "Skunks." The moniker stuck and now the Cal Western's logo is just that — a skunk.

One by one, the steamers on the roster were replaced entirely by diesels, and all passengers after 1925 were carried on the Skunks. But steam won't die! In 1965, steam passenger service was reintroduced, and steam engines are running again. Today, bright orange excursion trains are tugged by shining black engines (the "Super Skunks") through California's green redwoods, which thrive with new growth the more it rains.

The Logging Museum in Ft. Bragg features odd bits of lumbering engines on the site of the old fort. The Mendocino County Historical Museum can be found in Willits.

California Western RR, P.O. Box 907, Ft. Bragg, CA 95437, (707) 964-5651.

Equipment: Standard gauge, forty miles.

    Live: #45, 2-8-2 Baldwin Mikado (1924); #46, 2-6+6-2 Baldwin Mallet (1937); Three Baldwin diesels (also for local freight), #57 (1954), #55, #56 (1970); #100, Edwards (1925) and #300, American Car (1935) "Skunk" rail diesel cars.

    Rolling stock: Six coaches (ex-Erie RR and SP commute).

    Museum pieces: Two logging standard-gauge engines from the 1800s, track inspector's pedicycle.

Schedules: Skunk, daily, year-round, extra run mid-June to mid-Sept.

    Super Skunk, daily, second Sat. in June to second Sat. in Sept., also Memorial Day; Full and half-day trips, Ft. Bragg and Willits.

    Both trains operate out of Willits also, but some round trips necessitate an overnight layover in Ft. Bragg. Diesel traction is used east of Northspur (halfway point).

Fares: $9.90 (RT), $4.95 (5-11 years); half-day, $6.90/3.90.

Also: Museums (Ft. Bragg and Willits), shops, gift shop. (Author's note: The management of this road requires some encouragement to keep both locos in steam. Give it!)

Oregon, Pacific, & Eastern Railway, Cottage Grove, Oregon

An old favorite of railriding Northern Californians has been the Oregon, Pacific & Eastern's famous line, not too far from the California border. It has been often seen in movies — remember Lee Marvin in "King of the North?" But soaring insurance costs for excursion roads have put the OP&E's passenger division on the skids. If you want to help it out, give it your patronage. The more riders it has, the better it will do!

Their Railroad Town U.S.A. Museum is due for relocation. Normally, passengers are treated to a thirty-five-mile ride along the scenic Row River on tracks still used for lumbering.

Oregon Pacific & Eastern RR, P.O. Box 565, Cottage Grove, OR 97424, (503) 942-3368.

Equipment: Standard gauge, thirty-five miles.

    Loco: #19, "The Goose," 2-8-2 Baldwin Mikado (1914); diesel.

    Rolling stock: Several passenger cars.

Schedule: July 1-Labor Day at 2 P.M. Steam weekends, diesel weekdays.

Fares: $4.90/1.95 (5-11 years).

Also: Railroad museum with several other engines and cars.

Rail Rides, Miniatures, Northern California

Confusion Hill, Piercy, Mendocino County

Tucked away on a pine-covered hillside near the redwood parks of Highway 101 is a quiet little miniature train ride and the experience of Confusion Hill — so-named for the tourist attraction it houses there, which upsets the sense of balance. The train is a streamliner of the Arrow Development Corporation, and it pulls two cars. Eighteen-inch gauge, approximately three-inch scale. The ride is open May 1-Sept., 9-5, and the fares are $1.50/.75 (5-12 years).

Mr. Louie Attebury, Confusion Hill, Piercy, CA 95467, (707) 925-6456.

Maple Creek & Eastern Railroad, Cohasset, Butte County

At Cohasset, hidden in a pine forest near where no other railroad used to be, is an 18'' gauge miniature, the fancy of Mr. and Mrs. Don Sorenson and friends. Cohasset lies at the end of pavement of Cohasset Road,·NE, out of Chico.

Here the Sorensons *et al.* let many passengers, especially younger ones, ride free of charge over a half-mile loop. The two locos are kept in excellent condition, though it is rumored that the operators-engineers get more of a kick out of tinkering with "down" locos than with running them.

Mr. & Mrs. Donald Sorenson, Box 68, Cohasset Stage, Chico, CA 95926, (916) 343-4625.

Equipment:
Locos: #76, 0-6-0 1800s-style (1956); #101, 4-6-0 Sorenson Illinois Central-style streamliner (1971), both propane-fired steam; there's also an 0-4-0 gasoline-powered switcher.
Rolling stock: Five passenger gondolas, three flatcars, one boxcar, one cattle car, one caboose.
Also: Lakeside picnic facilities.

Schedule: Year-round, but by appointment — please call, especially for busloads of kids.
Fare: Free.

Operating Freight Roads and Their Shops/Yards

This junction, which is partly in a tunnel and partly on a high steel trestle, connects WP's main line with the 200-mile Western Pacific — Burlington Northern "Inside Gateway" that runs from Keddie, Calif. to Klamath Falls, Ore.

In all parts of California, there are a number of major railroad companies that serve the area. Since their yards and shops are usually to be found in more than one general location, I am categorizing them by town or area, rather than by the road itself.

On the other hand, the short lines don't wander about, so the reader will find them listed alphabetically by region. Readers can find those few that also give passenger service under the earlier listing of "Rail Rides."

Three Major Lines in Three Locations

Three major companies provide for the railroad needs of Northern California — the Southern Pacific, The Western Pacific, and the Burlington Northern. Although the BN, with fewer than eighty miles of track in California, is shorter here than some "short" lines, it *is* a major road in the Pacific Northwest (see p. 18).

Just over the California line, the lumbering center of *Klamath Falls, Oregon,* is also a rail center, serving California as well as Southern Oregon. Here is the major junction of the BN-WP's southbound "Inside Gateway" route with the SP's Cascade and Modoc lines. The town is also the terminus for the Weyerhauser Lumber Company's Oregon, California, & Eastern RR.

On the west side of town, the BN maintains a good-sized shop for its northbound trains and for its trains bound south to Stockton and Oakland. The BN also maintains a small yard at Nubieber, where it crosses State Highway 299.

Neatly bisecting Klamath Falls are the SP shops and yards. Here, the railfan can find several unusual pieces of equipment — for maintaining the right-of-way (R/W), as well as for dispensing winter's snows. Still in use is a 1926 steam rotary snowplow, a snowspreader, and a Jordan flanger (the railroad equivalent of a road grader).

A 1926 steam derrick (crane or "hook") is also maintained in operating condition. Whether or not we like to admit it, there are still numerous derailments, often in places that are inaccessible by road. Such misfortunes require a huge machine to put trains back on the track, and all railroads must have a crane available nearby.

Other features of SP's yards include two "high rail cars," or station wagons with extra steel wheels to quickly transport personnel to various sites along the line. At the center of the yards is SP's 1926 roundhouse, with a turntable.

Of historical note, the SP's Cascade line (used also by Amtrak) passes to the north through a spectacular loop in the upper Willamette Valley. To the southeast, the Modoc line joins the old Nevada, California, & Oregon RR route from Alturas to Wendel.

Perched along the high valley walls of the upper Sacramento River is the little town of *Dunsmuir*. Its former name was "Pusher," another word for the helper engines that the SP uses to push its longer trains over the mountains. Dunsmuir, then, is the site of the yards where helper engines are cut in and out for the 3.3-percent grade of the Siskiyou line (to Ashland, Oregon) and the 2.7-percent grades on the Cascade line. The old roundhouse is gone, but the turntable remains at the yards, as does a steam derrick and some snow-removal spreaders and flangers.

One of the more spectacular engineering features of this area is the double-decker road-railroad bridge over Lake Shasta. Interstate Highway 5 is on top, and the SP pokes in and out of tunnels on either end to occupy the lower deck. This 3,588-foot silver span was erected in 1941.

Before mounting the grade of the Feather River into the high Sierra, WP trains pass through the yards at *Oroville*. Once the main yards of the WP, these were moved to Stockton in 1969. The fine old roundhouse burned, but the turntable is there, serving the yards of the Solano Rail Car Company (a car repair outfit), which makes the area look a bit wrecked (or wretched). The WP's only crane is stationed here, with its work train at the ready.

Oroville, at the lower end, and Portola, at the upper, used to be the helper stations for traffic over the Beckwourth Pass; but now as many as seven ''road'' engines move entire trains from Stockton to Salt Lake City, needing no helpers and speeding up operations. This famous route was built with a 1-percent grade limit and has thirty-two tunnels, some of which have been opened up in recent years.

A recent, massive, modern addition to this line is the half-mile wide double-decker bridge over the West Branch of the Feather River at Lake Oroville. Highway 70 is on top; the WP emerges from a tunnel on the western end to occupy the lower deck.

Although now wholly owned by the SP, the Northwestern Pacific RR was once an independent line from San Francisco to Eureka-Arcata. The SF Bay termini were in Sausalito and Tiburon. But since the abandonment of the Bay ferries in the 1950s, the Sausalito tracks have lain abandoned, the Tiburon docks have rotted away, and the southern end of the former main line is only a spur from Corte Madera to Novato (Marin County), where a trunk line runs to the SP out of Vallejo.

However, to the north, the line normally handles two very long trains a day. Lumber makes up about 90-percent of the NWP's business. The largest part comes from the Humboldt Bay area, but other consignments arise from mills and other rail heads along the route.

The picturesque, 300-mile route snakes precariously through the forests of the Coast Range along the Russian and Eel Rivers, at times totally eschewing the company of highways, and passing through dozens of tunnels. In 1978, one of the road's major crises occurred when the ancient wooden timbers of one particularly long tunnel caught fire. Rails tarnished, and stranded trains sat idle for weeks until the stubborn fire was extinguished.

Division points (crew changes) and small yards are located in Willits and Eureka.

Two major antique pieces of the old NWP survive: the ferryboat Eureka (at San Francisco's Hyde Street Pier), and steamer #112, a sparkling 4-6-0 American (1908), soon to be seen at Sacramento's new Railroad Museum.

Short Lines

Since Northern California is a big lumber-producing region, it is no surprise that the nine short-line freight railroads listed here owe their existence to trees. Indeed, railroading itself owes some of its nomenclature to them, namely "trunk" and "branch" lines.

For a description of the California Western RR, which serves the Georgia-Pacific Lumber Company in Ft. Bragg, see the earlier listing (p. 50) under "Rail Rides."

Almanor Railroad, Chester-Westwood, Clear Creek Junction, Plumas County

Since the early 1940s, the Almanor RR has been strictly a logging railroad. It's a subsidiary of the Collins Pine Lumber Company, has thirteen and a half miles of track, and makes five weekly runs to its junction with the WP near Westwood. The headquarters and yards are in Chester, alongside beautiful Lake Almanor. Its one diesel, #166, is a fifty-ton General Electric, 1955 vintage.

Almanor RR, Box 796, Chester, CA 96020, (916) 258-2111.

In the yards, for winter use, is a most peculiar homemade, box-like, double-ended, orange snowplow — powered by Cummins-GE diesel electric.

Arcata & Mad River Railroad, Korbel-Arcata, Humboldt County

A sad-faced man in the Blue Lake Depot told me that the Arcata & Mad River's once-busy steam runs are no more — not even steam excursions. I've encountered such a dreary look only once before — when an SP official told me about the then-present state of the San Diego & Arizona Eastern RR (see p. 138).

Once a year, however, there are still *diesel* excursions during "Annie & Mary" days — the pet name for the A&MR — but that's a poor substitute for the little Shay that used to do the job.

I ran across an old-timer from Eureka over on the other side of the state in Martell, who related to me the following tale of the A&MR.

Once upon a time, the A&MR arrived regularly on Friday evenings down the middle of One Street in Eureka, its flatcars loaded with lumberjacks. As the train slowed to a halt, the cargo piled off into the saloons, gambling joints, and second-floor bordellos of One, Two, and Three Streets. At midnight on Sunday, the whistle blew — the signal for the lumberjacks to pile back on, empty-pocketed once again, ready for another week's work in the forests. These days, however, One, Two, and Three Streets are quieter. The A&MR quietly plods its rounds, serving eleven mills, hauling away their finished lumber for the houses of America.

The A&MR is owned by the Simpson Lumber company, and the yard is hidden in company sheds in Korbel.

The depot, and the railroad, too, are a state landmark.

Arcata & Mad River RR, Blue Lake, CA 95525, (707) 668-5753.

Equipment: Standard gauge, seven and a half miles.

Locos, diesel: Three forty-four-ton GEs (1940s).

Locos, steam: (Now property of the City of Arcata) #7, two-truck Shay (1917).

Diamond International, Red Bluff, Tehama County; Chico and Stirling City, Butte County

This is not exactly a "railroad" but, possessing its own tracks and engines, the Diamond International Corporation operates three quaint little diesels at its operations in Red Bluff, Chico, and Stirling City. Typical of these diesels is #796, an 0-4-0 GE twenty-five-ton switcher built in 1944, currently serving this wood-products company's operation in Red Bluff. The engineer says he can pull all of four or five loaded cars with his short little diesel, which is now equipped with a Cummins motor.

McCloud River Railroad, Mt. Shasta City-Burney and Hambone, Shasta County

There might be some argument, but in my opinion the McCloud River Railroad has the most beautiful setting of any railroad in California. Beginning at the foot of the frosty Mt. Shasta cone, it winds and twists, with a switchback, through ninety-seven miles of thick pine and fir forests of the McCloud River, to its junction with the Burlington Northern-Western Pacific at Hambone.

The McCRRR is a 99-percent logging road whose past, present, and future are tied completely to that industry. Its past began in 1897 as a logging road; it got its present name in 1907. Its present also includes a rather new roundhouse, shops, and even a hump in the yards. The offices occupy the huge, wooden, chalet-like station in McCloud that shadows several orange passenger cars, used on occasional steam excursions.

Well-tended timber farms of the region ensure the future of the McCRRR, although the fact that some of the more dense stands are logged out may portend a reduction in operations. Nevertheless, the sheer size of the timbering region that this railroad serves, as well as its deficiency of roads, can overcome the lack of diversification and the thinning of its natural resources.

The road has had some very interesting pieces of equipment, some of it now scattered. One item is a diminutive four-wheeled caboose, carefully preserved at the Sierra RR's museum in Jamestown. Another is the beautifully shaped, laminated, wooden snowplow, parked in the McCloud yards. Another of these artistic plows is displayed at Dunsmuir's Railroad Park.

McCloud River RR, McCloud, CA 96057, (916) 964-2141.

Equipment: Standard gauge, ninety-seven miles.

    Engines, diesel: Four 130-ton General Electrics (1969); **steam:** #24, 2-4-2 Baldwin Columbia (1925), used on occasional excursions.

    Rolling stock: Four hundred new boxcars, ninety-four older boxcars, two cabooses, flanger, wooden snowplow, executive car, three orange passenger cars for excursion.

Oregon, California, & Eastern Railroad, Klamath Falls-Bly, Klamath County, Oregon

So the Oregon, California, & Eastern RR didn't quite make it into California. California railfans like to know about it, anyway — it was featured in a recent (July 1977) edition of ''Railroad Magazine.'' The original OC&E of 1915 was planned to run east to meet the Nevada, California, & Oregon (see p. 19) at Lakeview, Oregon, but its backers ran short of cash before the hookup was made. Nevertheless, it kept its name. (The Frisco RR never made it there, either.)

After a while, the ubiquitous SP bought it, but in January 1975 it once again became a separate railroad, under the auspices of the Weyerhauser Lumber Company.

The OC&E has a most unusual feature, shared only by its neighbor, the McCloud River RR — a switchback. Its long-neglected tracks are undergoing a major overhaul, and its newly acquired engines bear a coat of country-green paint.

Oregon, California, & Eastern RR, Klamath Falls, OR 97601, (503) 882-5596.

Locos: Two 130-ton Morrison-Knudsens and five other 130-tonners, ex-UP, all late 1950s.

Rolling stock: Six cabooses, ex SP.

Old Engine No. 25, sister to No. 24, still in McCloud, pulls up for a drink.

Pacific Lumber Company, Scotia, Humboldt County

Very few California lumber companies maintain their own railroads now, but the PLC is one of them. Its traffic these days, however, involves hauling its finished lumber products directly to the NWP (SP) main line nearby.

Not many lumber companies have a fine museum or public plant tours, but the PLC has both. I was rather startled to also find a fine steam engine parked at the ready in a spic and span roundhouse — few lumber companies have one of those still around. Not only that, but the PLC is carefully preserving for posterity the last engine of the Mill Valley & Mt. Tamalpais RR (see p. 28) in its logging museum.

Pacific Lumber Company, Scotia, CA 95565, (707) 764-2222.

Equipment: Standard gauge, ten miles.

On display: #9, two-truck Heisler (1920), ex-MV&MTRR.

Live, steam: #29, 2-6-2 Baldwin Prairie (1910), serviceable storage.

Live, diesel: #101, #102, #103 all 80-ton GEs (1956); #104, #105 both 120-ton Baldwins (1945), both now for sale.

Rolling stock: Ninety-five lumber flatcars, 150 logging flats, five tankcars, one caboose, steam crane, railcar.

Also: Plant tours, logging museum, picnic facilities.

Quincy Railroad, Quincy, Plumas County

Quincy, like Yreka, is a town the big railroads bypassed on their way to somewhere else. In 1907, the Western Pacific put its busy transcontinental line up the Feather River, but Quincy lay just five miles too far off the best route.

After suffering at the hands of a succession of unscrupulous promoters, Quincy finally found some with scruples. In 1909, it got its five-mile track laid across a Sierra meadow to the WP.

The rushing auto traffic of Highway 70 passes through Quincy, not even crossing the tracks. To find the Quincy Railroad, you must first find its owner, the Sierra Pacific Industries lumber mill. Fortunately, in such a little town this is not a difficult task. The two small diesels of the QRR (not to be confused with the old Chicago, Burlington, & Quincy) reside in a small shed.

Across the street in the fairgrounds is an old engine of the Feather River Short Line Railroad, which once ran lumbering duty on the Sierra Nevada Wood and Lumber Company's Hobart Estate Railroad (Hobart Mills, California) and later carried excursions about the fairgrounds. This little engine sits at the head of a small mixed train, going nowhere. Even the Quincy Junction station is gone. But the QRR lives on, doing its lumbering duty daily.

Quincy Railroad, Sierra Pacific Industries, Quincy, CA 95971, (916) 283-2840.

Equipment: Standard gauge, five miles.

Locos, diesel: #3, forty-four-ton GE (1945), serviceable storage; #4, ninety-nine-ton GE (1941).

On display: in fairgrounds across street; Feather River Short Line #8, 2-6-2 Baldwin (1907), ex-Hobart Southern RR (1932-1937).

A one-time only nostalgic jaunt on Quincy Railroad's Old Engine No. 2, which took place in 1951.

Yreka Western Railroad, Yreka-Montague, Siskiyou County

We've seen all the movies in which the anxious town fathers attempt to cajole or even bribe the sharp-eyed, Richard Widmark-type railroad executive into bringing the fast-expanding railroad through *their* settlement. Well, that really happened right here in California, several times in fact. Inevitably, a few towns wound up bypassed, like Yreka in 1857 and Quincy in 1907; but both these towns did something about it.

Yreka, ghosting away in 1857 after the gold boom had withered, figured that a railroad could keep it from dying altogether. Around 1868, the SP's Oregon & California line had stranded Yreka six miles off to the west. So the town decided to found its own railroad — and in August 1887, the construction began, accompanied by bells, bands, and booms of gunpowder. By January 1889, the nine-mile line was officially opened.

For many years, the line had far more than its share of problems just keeping itself on the track. Schemers wanted to extend it physically — several mountainous miles into the Scott Valley — as well as financially, beyond its means.

Finally, on April 7, 1906, a San Francisco firm with great plans bought the road — eleven days before the great earthquake. The firm was destroyed, and the great plans with it.

Nevertheless, through human and roadbed washout, and despite the drain on its passenger service that the auto and bus caused, the Yreka Western Railroad stayed on. Decrepit trackage caused one observer to speculate that the train runs were "made more on the ground than on the rail."

In 1935, happier times were imminent. Track was repaired, and the financial house was put in order. Business was expanded to new lumber companies. And Yreka grew. The line went diesel in 1958, but kept two steam locomotives, one of which it still has.

A genuine and deep railroading instinct present in short-line railroaders has allowed this line to survive. It has been neither scrapped nor swallowed by the giants.

Today, the tiny Yreka Western prospers under the shadow of Mt. Shasta, serving lumbering and other local interests with two diesels and a fleet of forty-seven handsome boxcars. Once in a while, its president, Willis Kyle, gives local kids or execs a thrill with a ride in an old observation car to the SP junction at Montague.

Yreka Western RR, Yreka, CA 96097, (916) 842-4146.

Equipment: Standard gauge, eleven miles of track.

Locos, diesel: #602, GM (1952); #1172, Alco (1940), ex-UP; #1171, Alco (1940), ex-UP (not in service).

Locos, steam: #18, 2-8-2 Baldwin Mikado (1914) (not in service).

Rolling stock: #13, observation car; #409 observation car; half-open caboose, ex-McCloud River RR; forty-seven boxcars.

Also: Siskiyou County Museum, historic downtown Yreka, Mt. Shasta.

Local Railroadiana

Steamers on Display

There are a number of old steam engines in the northern part of the state that may be viewed by the general public. Some are in railroad yards, but most are in public parks. To examine those in private railroad yards, you must usually obtain permission from the yardmaster.

Alturas, *Rachel Dorris City Park*. An engine, gift of SP, #2718, 2-8-0 Baldwin (1904). It once ran on the Modoc branch and former NCO line. Cottage Grove (Oregon). See Oregon Pacific & Eastern RR.

Dunsmuir, *Dunsmuir RR Park*, at Castle Crags. Willamette Steel & Iron Company. Shay-type locomotive (1929) (built in Portland); also McCloud River RR flanger and snowplow. Friends of the 1727. SP #1727, 2-6-0 Baldwin Mogul (1901), in restoration.

Eureka, *Ft. Humboldt Logging Museum*. Bear Harbor & Eel River #1, "Bear Harbor Guppy," 0-4-0T Marshultz & Cantrell (SF) Dolbeer (1892); Elk River Mill & Lumber Company #1, "Falk Guppy," 0-4-0T Marshultz & Cantrell (1890), both under working restoration. Also, a logging car with double-flanged wheels and wooden rails.

Sequoia Park. Hammond-California Redwood Company #15, 2-8-2 Baldwin, in poor condition.

Ft. Bragg. See California Western RR.

Klamath Falls (Oregon), *Veterans Park*. SP #2579, 2-8-0 Baldwin Consolidation (1940). Southern Pacific yards. Steam derrick (1926); steam rotary snowplow.

Oroville, *Hewitt Park*. WP #164, 0-6-0 American switcher (1919); Feather River Railway Company #1, three-truck Lima Shay (1921), ex-Georgia Pacific Lumber Company.

Quincy, *Plumas County Fairgrounds*. See Quincy RR.

Scotia. See Pacific Lumber Company.

Yreka. See Yreka Western RR.

The Dolbeer was a locomotive invented in California by a logging engineer. It is a geared engine, often called a prototype of the Shay and Heisler (see p. 44).

Restaurants and Shops

Dunsmuir, *Dunsmuir Railroad Park*, "Caboose Car Steak House." Beloved project of Bill Murphy, this restaurant/museum is made up of several cars, including a Wells Fargo freight car. Outside are a Shay-style Willamette and other interesting pieces of equipment. (Closed Mon. and Tues.)

Eureka, *Old Town*, "Inside Track Boutique," 222 One St. is in an old passenger car.

Oroville, *Depot Restaurant*, an old WP depot.

Yreka, "Brownie's Diner," 1260 S. Main, is in a Yosemite Valley RR passenger car of 1910 vintage.

Museums

Eureka, *Ft. Humboldt Logging Museum*. (See p. 60).

Fortuna (Humboldt County), *Depot Museum in Rohner Park*. The old Northwestern Pacific's Fortuna Depot holds relics of earlier days. Open daily, 12-5, year-round.

Fort Bragg, *Georgia-Pacific Logging Museum* at California Western RR depot. Open weekdays; several engines outside.

Scotia, *Pacific Lumber Company Museum*. Open daily, year-round. Photos of early logging days, site of Mt. Tam RR's #9 engine.

Willits, *Mendocino County Historical Museum*.

Yreka, *Siskiyou County Museum*, 910 S. Main St. Local history of Yreka Western and Southern Pacific and Mt. Shasta area.

Private Collections

Scattered about the state are a number of private collections of working trains. Here are three that occasionally offer excursions to interested railfans. The owners request that you contact them before you arrive.

Feather River & Western Railroad, Portola, Plumas County

The owner of this very short line, Norman Holmes, runs occasional excursions on his one-quarter mile of track on his own ranch. The FR&W is about one mile east of Portola, on Highway 70.

Loco: #1, thirty-five-ton 0-4-0 Plymouth.

Rolling stock: Caboose #645, workcar, and boxcar, all ex-WP, and a small track motorcar.

Humboldt Northern Railroad, McKinleyville, Humboldt County

In long, chicken-farm sheds, where once a rooster could be heard crowing, now one is likely to hear a whistle blowing. The sheds are now a "stable" of fine, polished, narrow-gauge locomotives and railroad cars. These pieces have been collected and maintained since 1950 in this town, the site of the old Humboldt Northern, by Mr. and Mrs. Henry Sorensen and friends.

Carefully stashed away for "home use" and an occasional railway club excursion are, on half a mile of three-foot-gauge track:

Locos, steam: Branch Mint (N. Dakota) RR #1, "Natalie," 0-4-0 Porter (1906); Mattole Lumber Company #1, 0-4-2T Vulcan (1908); HN #6, 0-4-2T Baldwin (1929) ex-Japan; (disassembled) two-truck Lima Machine Works Shay (1887); **diesel:** #5, five-ton Plymouth yard switcher.

Rolling stock: Arcata & Mad River combine (originally 45½" gauge), four flats, one tankcar, one log hauler, one speeder, one set (very rare) of "disconnect trucks," which consists of only two trucks and an adjustable center beam (for hauling logs).

The Duke of Wellington (1769-1852):
"It is a mistake to build railroads because they only encourage the common people to move about needlessly."

Klamath & Hoppow Valley Railroad, Klamath, Del Norte County, CA

The most northwestern rails in California lie in the town of Klamath and thread through two lumber mill operations. Having lain dormant for a few years, the rails of Gus Peterson's lumber company railroad may someday be polished once again by steam.

Access to the Klamath & Hoppow Valley RR is near Highway 101, where it crosses the tidewater of the Klamath River. Trees grow fast here, and lumbering has slowed a bit, so there will be forests to clear-cut for some time. But for now, amid the plumes of smoke and steam characteristic of the California northwest, the K&HV continues to exist, if only intermittently.

Klamath & Hoppow Valley RR, Gus Peterson, owner, Klamath, CA 95548, (707) 482-3102.

Equipment: Standard gauge, about two miles.

Locos (wood-burning steam): #10, three-truck Heisler (1912); #17, 2-8-2T Alco (1929).

Rolling stock: Two cabooses for passengers.

Also: Some relics of logging railroad equipment; current operations of the Peterson and Simpson Lumber Companies.

An Artifact

At the settlement of Storrie, forty miles above Oroville on the North Fork of the Feather River, the tracks and sheaves of a fantastically-inclined cable car rust away. The cable and car, which are long gone, ran almost a mile up a nearly 45-degree mountain slope to service the siphon pipes of Pacific Gas and Electric's Bucks Creek Powerhouse. The powerhouse and railroad were built in the 1920s, but the cable service was abandoned when a road and helicopters provided better access to the summit.

Hobby Shops

Northern California is not notable for a large number of railroading hobby shops. You must go to San Francisco and especially Los Angeles for that. But here are two that cater to train fans:

Oroville: The Whistle Stop, 1900 Oro Dam Blvd.

Redding: Toy Depot, Downtown Redding Mall.

San Francisco Bay-Sacramento Area

S an Francisco is rapidly becoming a center of interest in rails, both old and new. The most exciting impetus for reactivating the "old" came in 1964, when the National Park Service declared San Francisco's venerable (1873) cable car system a national historic landmark. But as early as 1952, the cable cars had become part of the "Muni," San Francisco's pet name for the Municipal Railway system of streetcars, trolley buses, and buses. And as any visitor can tell you, San Francisco still respects its streetcars, some of whose routes antedate the cables.

Apparently, San Francisco has always been enthusiastic about rails. On the opening day of the Muni's first own line (A-Geary) in 1921, there were crowds, bands, firecrackers, speeches by Mayor (Sunny Jim) Rolph, and 20,000 jubilant riders at 5¢ a head. This scene occurred over and over, up to the inauguration of the N line in 1928.

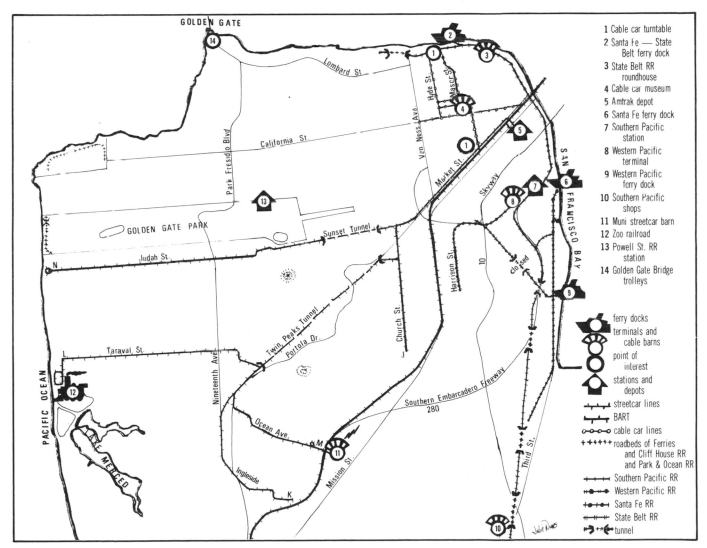

1 Cable car turntable
2 Santa Fe — State Belt ferry dock
3 State Belt RR roundhouse
4 Cable car museum
5 Amtrak depot
6 Santa Fe ferry dock
7 Southern Pacific station
8 Western Pacific terminal
9 Western Pacific ferry dock
10 Southern Pacific shops
11 Muni streetcar barn
12 Zoo railroad
13 Powell St. RR station
14 Golden Gate Bridge trolleys

ferry docks terminals and cable barns
point of interest
stations and depots
streetcar lines
BART
cable car lines
roadbeds of Ferries and Cliff House RR and Park & Ocean RR
Southern Pacific RR
Western Pacific RR
Santa Fe RR
State Belt RR
tunnel

Rail Rides, Standard and Narrow Gauges

Working quietly, but with whistles wailing, a growing number of dedicated railfans are acquiring, rebuilding, and restoring dozens of old locomotives and rolling stock. These selfless workers are offering their hobbies to the public at ridiculously low fares for rides.

At the same time, "new" rails are also enjoying a great boom. The Muni is keeping up with the rest of the transportation world — the Market Street car lines are now underground, and miles of surface track have been rebuilt to accommodate the fast, new, caterpillar-like cars that were designed to be used by both San Francisco and Boston.

Since 1972, the shiny new cars of the Bay Area Rapid Transit Authority (BART) have been dashing or dallying about the Bay Area's far-flung districts at 0-75 m.p.h. Ah, BART — an overcomputerized system that apparently was not designed by a railroad man. There are no stubs for out-of-service trains, the manual control system for slowed operation is poor; and other constant problems retard commuters as much as twenty to thirty minutes each day. One wag has suggested that BART should be named the Charles E. Bolton Memorial Railroad. Charles E. Bolton — a.k.a. Black Bart — was one of the first Californians to hold up passengers. Nevertheless, when functioning well, BART offers a pleasant and pretty ride. On those off-days when all rides are 50¢, it gathers full loads of the curious.

At Amtrak's Oakland station, eight trains a day arrive and depart for both borders and the Atlantic shore. A new service to Monterey is planned to open soon.

About the only diminishing rail service around the Bay is that of the rail ferries that go from San Francisco to Richmond and Oakland, across the Bay. There are only two left, and they operate only at night. Heavy industry is relocating away from San Francisco so fast that the mate of the *Las Plumas* told me, "Pretty soon we'll be carrying only typewriters and paper."

Let's take a look at some of the myriad rail features of today and yesterday that are all around us.

The Cable Cars

There are thirty-nine cable cars, and if you ride all three lines — Nos. 59 (Powell-Mason), 60 (Powell-Hyde), and 61 (California) — from end to end, you will have traveled ten miles. The cable cars sleep at Washington and Mason Streets on the upper level of the Cable Car Museum — where there's a dispatcher's clock in Chinese, and a cable car elevator.

The oldest of the bunch was born in 1886, the youngest in 1907. Since they are part of the Muni, the ride is, so far, only a quarter, and transfers are given and received cheerfully.

Without looking too hard, you'll find two distinct types of cable cars. One type is maroon and rather long and has "grips" at both ends. These run only on California Street and date from 1907 (after the earthquake). The other variety is green and yellow and macaroni. These have to be turntabled around at the ends of the line, because they are strictly a one-ended operation. They run on the two Powell Street lines and date from 1886 to 1907.

For more information, see Cable Car Museum, p. 88.

An early photo of the Palace Hotel showing three of San Francisco's rail systems.

The Streetcars of the San Francisco Municipal Railway

All 115 streetcars retire to their shops and barn at Geneva Avenue and San Jose Boulevard, out in the Mission district. It would take several hours to ride the five lines — J-Church (to Mission Dolores), K-Ingleside (to City College or the barn), L-Taraval (to the zoo), M-Oceanview (to SF State University), and N-Judah (to Golden Gate Park and Ocean Beach). If you did, you'd go through two tunnels and traverse seventy miles.

You'll find three of the five kinds of streetcars in daily use, but those three may be camouflaged by similar paint jobs. The ancient No. 1 prowls about to ''Nowhere'' under charter on weekends, and No. 0131 is a repair car that is used only when there's trouble.

Some streetcar data:

No. 1 (K-Line designation) (1912, W.L. Holman Company) is maroon and gray. With its huge cowcatchers, retractable steps, and a sign reading ''Nowhere in Particular,'' it is quite distinctive.

No. 0131 (1914, Jewett Car Company) is bright yellow with red stripes, and is used as a repair and wrecker car because its motors are very strong.

These two powerful cars, remnants of a fleet dubbed ''O'Shaugnessy Tanks,'' are typical of those once used on the steeper routes that are now serviced by the electric trolley buses.

''Presidential Conference Cars'' (products of Westinghouse, General Electric, and Bethlehem Steel) are green and yellow or, occasionally, Muni's new orange and white. Some models, Nos. 1006-1015 (1948), were built with four doors and lights on both ends for operation in both directions; but now the streetside doors are welded shut. Other models (from 1946 and 1951) are single-ended and two-door, reflecting the ten-revolutionary idea of one-man operation. The youngest cars (at least to the Muni — 1944) are maroon and yellow (from Kansas City *via* Toronto), and were brought to San Francisco in 1974. They are seldom in use.

Incidentally, old tower car #0304 sits in the shops, used for occasional wire work in tunnels and other places that are inaccessible by truck.

The first LRV's (''light rail vehicles,'' so the admen call them) are promised for 1979 service, and will bear numbers 1200-1299. Already car #1222 is testing routes.

Streetcar rides are only 25¢, transfers are free, and the cars run from 7 A.M. to 11 P.M., 365 days a year (more or less). For schedule and route information, call (415) 673-MUNI.

San Francisco Municipal Railway, 949 Presidio Ave., San Francisco, CA 94118, (415) 673-MUNI.

Only in San Francisco can you still see an operating streetcar line.

Antique Streetcars and Interurbans

If you'd like an electrified ride on a genuine antique streetcar or interurban in an open rural setting, try the *California Railway Museum* in Rio Vista. On running days, they bring out two cars from their collection of some twenty-eight cars of this category, and once in a while there's a parade of *all* their operable stock.

For details of schedules, fares and equipment, see p. 89.

Bay Area Rapid Transit (BART)

It's quite a thrill to zip under 135 feet of water of the San Francisco Bay on the spacious, shiny cars of BART at 75 m.p.h. BART is still being expanded, eventually to San Jose and possibly Sacramento (if Amtrak doesn't do it first), but even now the system is seventy miles long and has thirty-four stations. Sooner or (probably) later, there will be 450 cars; however, right now you can travel, say, the forty-five miles from Concord to Fremont in only fifty-seven minutes. Don't try that in your car!

A BART train consists of from two to ten cars, which are parked at four different locations around the Bay; shops are in Hayward. The cars are a product of Rohr Industries.

BART runs daily; the last trains depart about 11 P.M.

The longest run (maximum one-way fare) is Fremont to Daly City and costs $1.45. For schedules and routes, call (415) 788-BART.

Bay Area Rapid Transit District, 800 Madison St., Oakland, CA 94607, (415) 465-4100.

Diesel Passenger Service

There are two ways to sightsee the Bay Area by diesel. One route is to the South Bay by Southern Pacific. There are twenty-two SP commute trains leaving and arriving in San Francisco daily, using twenty-three diesel units. All the trains are equipped with fine double-decker cars that offer good vistas of the Bay and the many communities to the south. Trains run every day, all year. In 1863, the fare was $2.50. Today, the one-way fare from San Francisco to San Jose is only $3.20 (cheaper for kids). The SP schedule and fares phone is (415) 981-4700; for public relations information, dial (415) 362-1212.

Amtrak has eight departures and arrivals every day for Canada, Mexico, Chicago-New York, and Yosemite-Bakersfield. For a good day of sightseeing, though, you don't have to go that far. Day trips to nearby towns are both cheap and easy. Free buses leave San Francisco to meet all trains at the Oakland passenger station. We're all hoping to see the Del Monte Express reopen soon. With the support of Caltrak, the new state system, the Del Monte will go to Fisherman's Wharf in Monterey.

The fare on the daily Oakland to Sacramento run over SP tracks is $6.50 for adults and half fare for 2-11 years (reservations required). The daily run over Santa Fe tracks from Oakland to Stockton is only $5.75 (2-11 years, half fare) and no reservations are required.

Amtrak's Western telephone is (800) 648-3850. There are Bay Area stations in Sacramento, Davis, San Francisco, Stockton, Martinez, and San Jose.

Great America Park, Santa Clara

This "theme" amusement park in Santa Clara is surrounded by the Great America Scenic Railway, a mile-long, full-scale, thirty-six-inch, narrow-gauge road. Each of two trains pulls six large covered passenger gondolas. The engines, #16 and #19, built in 1976 by Custom Fabricators of Johnson City, Tennessee, are 1800s-style, but they are diesel-electric powered — with oil storage in the "boiler" and power in the tender! In only 150 days of operation, these trains carry nearly one million passengers on their routes.

In addition, two full-scale, battery-powered, California cable-style trams run about the grounds on half a mile of track. In the yards is an antique 0-4-0 Cummins diesel switcher.

Park admission to all rides is $8.95/7.95 (4-11 years). Rides run on weekends in spring and fall, daily in summer.

Marriott's Great America, Santa Clara, CA 95052, (408) 988-1776.

Big, Live, Steam Engines

Want to ride on a real, honest-to-goodness live steam train? Aside from occasional, specially organized trips by railfan clubs, there are four places within three hours of San Francisco where regular trains operate. Year-round weekend and daily summer service is to be found in Felton, near Santa Cruz, at the Roaring Camp and Big Trees Narrow Gauge Railroad depot. A group of dedicated trainmen maintain a stable of fine locomotives (and two diesels). The steamers are from various lumber yards, mines, and sugar plantations. For over an hour, one of these worthies chugs at walking speed up a mountainside of redwoods, over switchback, and then over corkscrew trestles to a picnic site. (For details, see p. 92).

On summer weekends, the antique (and modern) Sierra Railroad in Jamestown operates two-hour excursions on big Baldwin chuffers with roomy coaches. This road offers everything; from a two-hour ride past a huge lumberyard to an all-evening dinner trip (in which perfume and long dresses mix with smoke and sooty overalls). Almost anytime you see a train in a movie or on TV ("High Noon," "Petticoat Junction," etc.), chances are it's one of theirs. The Sierra RR has been in independent operation since 1897. (See p. 98).

If a day-long outing through unpopulated forests sounds enticing, take yourself to Ft. Bragg for the Super Skunks of the California Western Railroad. This ride is a true nostalgia trip, even if you weren't alive seventy years ago. This railroad has the orangest of coaches pulled by the blackest of engines through the greenest of redwoods. For a different treat, they also have antique rail diesel cars that go daily over the same forty-mile route. (For details of this road, see p. 50).

The nearest live steam to San Francisco is found right at the foot of the Richmond Bridge in Richmond on the Castro Point Railway. On the first Sunday of every month, the Pacific Locomotive Association hauls out one or two ancient steam engines from their large collection, and offers rides along the beautiful San Francisco Bay shore for the absurd price of nothing. You can stay and ride all day, if you like. In late summer, when fire danger is high, the fine old rolling stock is still used, but the fire department requires them to use an antique diesel engine instead of the steamers. (Details about this railroad can be found on p. 90).

Here's a picture of what might be in store for you when you visit one of the steam railroads.

Rail Rides, Miniature Steam

Every steam fan will want to sample each of the five miniature live steam railroads of the Bay Area, because each line offers something unique. From the wine country to parks to high scenic vistas, all over the area you can find these powerful little engines pulling loads of delighted adults as well as children.

Billy Jones Wildcat Railroad, Los Gatos

This road is named for the benefactor who, many years ago, "rescued" the line from Los Angeles. It is located in Vasona Lake County Park in Los Gatos (Lake Avenue exit from Highway 17). The antique (1905) engine was built for a Venice (Ca.) real estate venture. The ride is about fifteen minutes for a good scenic view of the park. Eighteen-inch gauge, four-inch scale.

Billy Jones Wildcat RR, P.O. Box 1860, Los Gatos, CA 95030, (408) 354-8320.

Equipment:

Locomotive: #2, 2-6-2 Johnson Machine Works Prairie-style (1905).

Rolling stock: Six passenger gondolas, two flatcars, one boxcar, and one caboose; some original equipment.

(Note: Engine #3, 2-6-0 Coit Mogul-type (1901) is currently under restoration.)

Schedule: Easter-Memorial Day, Sat. 11 A.M.-5:37 P.M., Sun. 12-5:37 P.M.; Summer, 11 A.M.-5:37 P.M., Tues.-Sun.; Labor Day-Oct. 15, weekends same as spring.

Fare: 50¢/10 for $3.50 (under 2, free).

Also: RR turntable and shops, park picnic area, refreshments.

Repairing the locomotive on the Billy Jones Wildcat Railroad.

Calistoga Steam Railroad, Calistoga

Any railfan taking a trip to the wine country shouldn't pass up this living antique miniature, located on the Silverado Trail (Highway 607, near Highway 128) in Calistoga. The engine is in magnificent condition, and was one of those used at the San Francisco Panama-Pacific Exposition in 1915. The run is two and a quarter miles through fields beside vineyards and up a good ''mountain'' grade. The railroad may soon go directly into Calistoga to the old SP depot there. Nineteen-inch gauge, four-inch scale.

Calistoga Steam RR, Silverado Trail at Brannan St., Calistoga, CA 94515, (707) 942-5353.

Equipment:

Locomotive: #1913, 4-6-2 McDermott Pacific-style (1913).

Rolling stock: Four passenger gondolas (Overfair type), one of which is original 1915 equipment.

(Note: Engine #1912, sister to #1913, is currently in restoration in the Redwood Valley Shops.)

Schedule: Sept.-June 15, 12-5 daily, weekends; June 15-Aug., 12-5, check with RR for Moonlight and Wine Train Specials.

Fare: $1.50/$1.00 (5-12 years).

Also: Refreshment stand, checkers.

An outing, complete with flags flying, on the Calistoga Steam Railroad.

Redwood Valley Railway, Berkeley

The neatest little *coal-fired* steam train around is this one on Grizzly Peak Road, Tilden Park, Berkeley. Built by Erich Thomsen in 1965, the engine is a feisty, shiny, 1800s type, pulling a variety of special cars. The half-hour ride is only 50¢, and is entirely self-supporting! Fifteen-inch gauge, five-inch scale.

Redwood Valley Ry, Tilden Park, Berkeley, CA 94705, (415) 531-9300.

Equipment:

Locomotives: #2, 0-4-0 gasoline switcher (1942) for yard work; #4, 2-4-2 Thomsen Columbia-style (1965) (coal); #11, 4-6-0, oil-fired steamer.

Rolling stock: Five passenger gondolas, flatcar, coalcar, caboose (all 1966-68). Also in use, ten freight four-wheelers and two roofed passenger cars.

Schedule: 11-6 Sat., Sun., and holidays, all year, and seven days a week mid-June to Labor Day (Mon-Fri, 1-6).

Fare: 60¢, five for $2.40.

Also: The myriad attractions of Tilden Park.

The Bay Area Air Pollution Control Board granted a variance for this coal-fired locomotive.

San Francisco Zoo Steam Train

This little engine is the grandparent of all the Bay Area miniatures, and has even seen service as a mine engine. Presently it is on display in the Elephant House while a new and much longer route is being constructed. Twenty-two-inch gauge, approximately five-inch scale.

San Francisco Zoo, San Francisco, CA 94116, (415) 661-1553.

Equipment:

Locomotive: #251, 4-4-0 Cagney American-style (1893).

Rolling stock: Three passenger gondolas, one work car.

Zoo Schedule: 10-5, year-round.

Fare: Admission to the grounds, $1.00/50¢ (2-15 years).

Also: Other attractions of the zoo include SP #1294, an 0 6 0 switcher (1924), and a California cable car on display in the Children's Zoo — both for climbing on.

This 1893 engine is currently sitting in the Elephant House at the zoo waiting for new tracks.

Sonoma Gaslight & Western Railroad, Sonoma

Train Town, on Highway 12, just south of Sonoma, is the site of this unique miniature railroad and miniature gold-mining town. A run of fifteen minutes through one and a quarter miles of track in a beautifully landscaped tract is a distinct pleasure for railfans — and it's right at the entrance to the wine country. Fifteen-inch gauge, three-inch scale.

Sonoma Gaslight & Western RR, P.O. Box 656, Sonoma, CA 95476, (707) 938-3912.

Equipment:

Locomotives: #5212, 4-6-4 Alco Hudson-style (1937) built by American in Schenectady as an exact replica of a NY Central Hudson loco; #1, 2-6-0 Winton Mogul-style (1960); diesel rail car (gasoline).

Rolling stock: Five passenger gondolas; seven freight cars including a caboose; two scale coaches.

Schedule: 10:30 A.M.-5:30 P.M., weekends and holidays, all year; daily, June 17-Labor Day.

Fare: $1.50/$1.00 (2-12 years) (possibly higher in 1979).

"Well, what are the orders for today, sir?"

Rail Rides, Non-Steam Miniatures

Children's Fairyland, Oakland

Located at Lake Merritt, Oakland, and operates daily in summer, on weekends and school holidays Nov. 1-Mar 1, and Wed.-Sun. the rest of the year. The Bay Area's most whimsical train is called the Jolly Trolly. It was built by Jack Francis, an Oakland policeman, around 1954. 40¢/30¢ for a long, ten-minute ride. (415) 452-2259.

Frontier Village, San Jose

At 4885 Monterey Road. Uses a nineteenth-century-style 30'' gauge, 7'' scale, Corvair-powered train with open gondolas for park transportation over its .8 mile. It was built by Arrow Development in 1960. Park admission for all rides is $5.95 (over 3 years). Frontier Village is open all day, daily from Memorial Day-Labor Day, and on weekends and school holidays year-round. (408) 225-1500.

Great America Park, Santa Clara

This park has, in addition to its narrow-gauge railroad and trolleys (see p. 68), three rail "high rides." All utilize a unique three-wheel grip on pipe-like rails. One system, "Willard's Whizzer," is electrically self-propelled. Another, the exciting corkscrew "Turn of the Century," is trundled to the top of the track by a cable-chain. The "Tidal Wave" is propelled by the most unusual system on Central California rails — a catapult. Park admission for all rides is $8.95/7.95. (408) 988-1776.

Harvey West Municipal Park, Santa Cruz

Features two items of rail interest. The Sierra & Golden West Railway Company runs its "Eureka #1," an 0-4-0 Kohler engine of 1890s style (1968) on a one-half-mile ride for 50¢. Daily June-Sept. on weekends and holidays Easter-June and Sept.-Oct. Sixteen-inch gauge, four-inch scale. (408) 423-1860. Also in the park is SP's #1298, 0-6-0 of 1920s vintage, for climbing on.

Howarth Park, Santa Rosa

Located in the "Big K (Kiwanis) Land," has a Kansas-made, gasoline-powered replica of the Central Pacific #18 "C.P. Huntington" of 1863 style. Fifteen-inch gauge. Hours are 10-4:30 weekends, 15¢ for a quarter mile, five-minute ride. (707) 528-5115.

Kennedy Park, Hayward

They have an 1800s-style engine, #3, 4-4-0 Ray Maker American-style (1975). It is powered by a Chevrolet-6 motor, chain driven. Track loop is half a mile for a five-minute ride around the park, and operates on school holidays and weekends 11-4:30, and daily in summer. The fare is 35¢. The train is three-inch scale, twenty-four-inch gauge. (415) 881-6745.

Land Park, Sacramento

This park offers rides on a thirty-year-old #1024, 4-4-2 nineteenth-century-style Hurlbut engine pulling four open gondolas. The ride is 30¢/20¢ (0-12 years) for three quarters of a mile. Open 11-5 daily in summer, and on weekends in winter. The gauge is an unusual fourteen and a half inch.

Nut Tree Railroad, Vacaville

A neat 1800s-style gasoline train shuttles year-round betwen the airport and a restaurant (winter 11-7, summer 9-9). The engine, #5, is from the Hurlbut Equipment Company (1959) and is mounted on twenty-inch-gauge track that passes through a beautiful garden. 50¢. (707) 448-6411.

Just ride around the grounds or go to the Vacaville Airport on the Nut Tree Railroad.

Oakland Zoo Railroad

Runs a New York Central streamliner miniature over a one-mile, twenty-four-inch gauge track with a spectacular view. The engine (1964) by Ray Maker is a chain-driven F-85 Olds, pulling four enclosed cars. Park admission is $1/car, $3/bus. 40¢/ride. Open year-round, 10-4. (415) 568-2470.

Santa's Village Faire, Scott's Valley

On Highway 17 near Santa Cruz, this attraction features a little old, old-style engine and three-four gondolas on a twenty-inch-gauge track on a three-to-four-inch scale. It was built by the Hurlbut Equipment Company in 1954.

Enjoy the Oakland Zoo and some of the best views of the San Francisco Bay, too.

Santa Cruz Beach-Boardwalk

Offers rides on its "Cave Trains," two electric-powered engines of the Arrow Development Corporation (1962) on a six-minute, 2,000-foot-long ride. But the most invigorating rail ride is the cable-gravity train called the "Giant Dipper" — the oldest wooden roller coaster in the western U.S. (1924). Its two trains travel a half-mile in two minutes. Nearby is the smaller, German-made coaster, "Jet Star." Fares: "Cave Train," $.60/.40 (to 12 years); "Dipper," $.80; "Jet Star," $.60. Schedules (weather permitting) are daily in summer, 11-11, and weekends in winter, 11-dark. (408) 423-5590.

The park operates year-round on weekends and holidays, and daily in the summer. Park admission is $1.00 + 50¢/ride, or $4.00 admission for all rides. (408) 438-2250.

Willow Pass Park, Concord

This park has a replica of an F-7 diesel with three passenger gondolas running half a mile for about five minutes around a children's park. The Miniature Train Company engine (1956) is one-fifth scale and sixteen-inch gauge. Fares are 50¢/40¢ (to 12 years). Open on weekends and holidays Jan.-June 10, and daily June 10-Labor Day (closed Dec.).

See also the Cal Expo monorail (p. 86).

Regional Commercial Freight and Transit Lines--Their Shops, Yards, Terminals, and Car Barns

Alameda Belt Line

Diesel shed, 2000 Thau, Alameda. Gets the ugly prize for neglect and deterioration.

Amtrak

San Francisco's East Bay (bus, once interurban) Terminal, 1st and Mission Streets; Del Monte Express may soon depart from the SP Depot; Oakland Depot (with abandoned interurban platform on second deck) at 16th and Wood Streets; also stations in Sacramento (Eye Street), San Jose (Alameda and Cahill), Davis, and Martinez; service yards at the Oakland SP yards.

Atchison, Topeka, & Santa Fe

Only a few blocks of tracks in San Francisco around China Basin; their yards in Richmond at Garrard and Standard include an antique roundhouse and turntable.

BART

Yards (hard to find) located in Hayward with RR connection (but with five-foot, six-inch gauge, compared to four-foot, eight-and-a-half-inch standard).

Cable Car Barn

Included area museum and turntable, at Washington and Mason Streets, San Francisco.

The Cable Car Museum, a powerhouse, and Muni's cable car barn — all in one place.

Central California Traction

Has an office and a tiny siding on Florin Perkins Road in Sacramento (shops in Stockton).

Howard Terminal Railroad

Its one diesel is kept at 95 Market Street in Oakland.

San Francisco Belt Railroad

Has a roundhouse for its switchers doing night duty at Chestnut and Embarcadero, San Francisco. The barge flats for loading the Santa Fe ferry at Fisherman's Wharf still bear the "State Belt" designation.

Car No. 1 tucked into the corner of Muni's streetcar barn.

Muni Streetcars

Included are No. 1 (1912) and the "old yeller" (1914). They can be seen at the shops at Geneva and San Jose Avenues, San Francisco. This facility is expanding across the street to accommodate the large, new streetcar fleet expected in 1979.

Oakland Terminal Railway

They park their one little diesel under Interstate 80 alongside Engineer Road, Oakland.

Southern Pacific

Commute Depot, 5th and Townsend Streets, San Francisco, is near a diesel service station; super tidy and clean yards, also for Amtrak, are at 7th and Wood Streets, Oakland; and a fine old roundhouse and turntable can be found at Stockton and Lenzer, San Jose.

Southern Pacific

Shops, roundhouse, turntable, and sometimes its steam crane, are at Geneva Avenue and Bayshore Boulevard, San Francisco. There also are miles of engine shops at Roseville, just NE of Sacramento. Nearby at Antelope is the SP's Pacific Fruit Express boxcar shops.

Western Pacific

Has diesel overnight parking and freight loading at 8th and Brannan Streets, San Francisco; yards are at 1407 Middle Harbor Road, Oakland. Once in a while you might see Burlington Northern or Union Pacific engines/cabooses on this line.

The Southern Pacific's Bayshore Yard and Shops, where you can sit on a hill and watch the daisies grow or the trains move around.

San Francisco Bay Short Lines

Alameda Belt Line Railroad and Oakland Terminal Railway

In the San Francisco East Bay are a pair of roads that, as fate would have it, must be mentioned in the same paragraph. Both are half-owned by the Western Pacific and the Santa Fe. Both are under the same overall supervision and maintenance. About the only thing different about them is that they are in two locations.

The Oakland Terminal is really the operating remnant of the old Key System. It began around 1942, doing strictly industrial switching around the Port of Oakland facilities. Today, it continues to do just that, on some twenty miles of track.

The Alameda Belt, acquired from the city of Alameda, became a private road in the 1920s until it was taken over by the WP and the Santa Fe. The two roads share two engines, which seem to be more or less interchangeable, and which are maintained at the Alameda shops and at the WP shops in Stockton.

Alameda Belt Line, shed, 2000 Thau, Alameda, CA, (415) 522-5280. Oakland Terminal RR, Engineer Rd., Oakland, CA, (415) 832-8464.

Locomotives: OT, 115-ton Alco (1944); ABL, 120-ton Baldwin (1946)

Howard Terminal Railroad, Oakland

This just might be the shortest short line in independent existence in California — and it's hiding in a corner of Oakland with only one and a half miles of track. The Howard Terminal Railroad was founded in 1917 to service the docks adjacent to the Howard Terminal at the foot of Market Street.

Once it had three steamers, but as the containers took over, operations were confined to boatless tenants. Its one sturdy diesel is enough for business now, hauling cars to and from the nearby SP and WP connecting lines.

Howard Terminal RR, 95 Market St., Oakland CA 94607, (415) 451-4722.

Loco: One forty-four-ton Whitcomb (1943). It's really unique — see it before it's phased out!

Leslie Salt Company, Newark, Alameda County

One of the more unusual railroad operations in California is the Leslie Salt Company's three salt-pan railroads. The process of obtaining salt from sea water made early use of solar energy (since 1950). The sea water is confined in large, low-lying ponds called "pans." To collect the salt, the company uses a large, tractor-like harvester to scrape it up and dump it into waiting, ore-type cars. The cars are placed on portable tracks in fifteen-foot sections, much like model-train tracks, that rest directly on the salt bed. The track is moved with each pass of the harvester.

In each of its three locations, the harvesting operation can take from two to four months, and goes on twenty-four hours a day. You can easily spot the locations, in Redwood City, Hayward, and Green Island (near Napa), by the enormous, glistening white salt piles nearby.

Hayward: Has about twenty miles of track, twenty-four-inch and thirty-inch gauge.

Redwood City and Napa: about two miles each, thirty-inch gauge.

Leslie Salt Company, 7200 Central Avenue, Newark, CA 94560, (415) 797-1820, and 295 Harbor Boulevard Redwood City, CA 94063, (415) 368-3120.

Equipment:

Locos (24''): Eleven Vulcan diesels, five-ton (1951), Hayward only; (30''): four Vulcans, five Caterpillars, four Brookvilles, all about five tons, all 1951, all interchangeable locations.

Salt cars: Two hundred and twenty ore-type dumpers.

Richmond Beltline Railroad, Contra Costa County

The Richmond Beltline is one of those vestiges of corporate controversies. Once independent, it now consists only of a few tracks owned jointly by the AT&SF and the SP, operated in five-year rotations by each. The tracks serve only the Standard Oil Company in Richmond and as access to the far more glamorous Castro Point Railway.

San Francisco Belt Railroad

Once upon a time, especially the time of the Second World War, the SF Belt did a booming business as the State Belt Railroad. Its few miles of track are confined to the Embarcadero of San Francisco, but they're still used on weekdays from 6 A.M. to 2 P.M. — a schedule designed to avoid the tourists who are slowly squeezing it out, as the wharf area becomes less industrial.

The SF Belt serves a few piers that still are used for commercial purposes, and a malting factory. It connects to the SP on Townsend Street on one end, and the Santa Fe's rail barge at Pier 43½ on the other. So that the engine won't weigh down the ferry approach, four barge flats are pushed in front of it while the barge is being loaded. These flats are usually stored in the yards at Jefferson Street.

There are plans afoot to convert this line into Muni transit lines up and down the Embarcadero. We'll wait and see.

San Francisco State Belt RR, Port Commission, Ferry Building, San Francisco, CA 94111, (415) 391-8417.

Equipment:

Locos: #23 and #25, 130-ton GE's (1940s).
Rolling stock: Four barge flats, labelled "State Belt."

Railroadiana

Distinctive Rail Engineering Features

The San Francisco Bay-Sacramento region abounds with a good sampling of the engineering feats of railroading — some large, some small, some unusual, some very familiar.

Docks:

Rail ferry (1910), of the Western Pacific are at 25th Street, San Francisco, adjacent to a city park and the Oakland Mole (no public access by land). The one remaining Bay rail ferry, the *Las Plumas* (1951), operates from 12 midnight to noon. The last San Francisco departure is about 5 A.M.

The San Francisco rail ferryboat *Las Plumas* just docking in the early morning after working all night.

Docks:

Railroad barge, called "moles," of the Santa Fe are to be found in San Francisco at Fisherman's Wharf at Pier 43 and south of China Basin at Pier 52. The Richmond Mole is a mile west of the Point Richmond Tunnel (accessible by car). The barge holds thirteen cars, which are tugged by a bright yellow ship of 1945 vintage, the *Paul P. Hastings*. Continuous operation.

Santa Fe's *Paul P. Hastings*, with its railroad barge tied up in San Francisco.

A bascule drawbridge over the San Joaquin River near Stockton.

Around the Bay and Delta

"Draw" bridges, railroad — there are nineteen of these. The seven true draw spans are: on 3rd St. over Mission Creek (China Basin) in San Francisco; over Madera Creek at Drake Blvd. in Greenbrae (Marin County); over the Middle River (AT&SF) in San Joaquin County; over the San Joaquin River (AT&SF) by Hwy. 4 in Stockton; an abandoned SP span over Georgiana Slough near Walnut Grove (San Joaquin County); a road-railroad draw in Vallejo to the Mare Island Naval station; there is another on Jefferson Blvd., West Sacramento, over the Port of Sacramento Channel.

The three lift bridges are by Tilden Ave. over the Oakland Channel in Alameda; the huge SP bridge over the Carquinez Strait in Martinez; and a span (now fixed) over the San Joaquin River alongside Hwy. 5 near Tracy.

The nine swing ("turn" or "axle") bridges are: over Petaluma Creek at Hwy. 101 in Petaluma (Sonoma County); 1 over San Antonio Creek by Hwy. 37 at Black Point (Marin-Sonoma Counties); over the Old River (AT&SF) (San Joaquin-Contra Costa Counties); over the San Joaquin River at the Naval Station in Stockton; the "I" St. double-decker over the Sacramento River in Sacramento; two over the South (S.F.) Bay (SP) alongside the Dumbarton (Hwy. 84) Bridge; the SP span over the Napa River to Green Island south of Napa; and at the ghost town of Drawbridge near Fremont (SP).

Funiculars

There are four funiculars (private) in the 700 block of Bay Street, San Francisco, some thirty years old, serving high, mid-block residences. Shadowbrook, in Capitola, has a half-block long public funicular of Dwan and Company, about 1958 vintage.

Monorail

The one Central California monorail is to be found at the California Exposition and State Fairgrounds in Sacramento. It operates only from mid-August to early September, 10 A.M.-10 P.M. It was built in 1960 by the California Minirail Corporation, and has four trains of eight cars each. Park admission is $2.50, and the ride is 75¢. (916) 641-2331.

cisco, one at Altamont Pass near Livermore, and one in Rodeo; three on the old Northwestern Pacific (SP) in Marin County — some disused; two BART (under the Oakland Hills and the San Francisco Bay); two Muni streetcar (Sunset, N-Line, and Twin Peaks, K-, L-, and M-Lines); one ex-streetcar (F-Stockton, now a trolleybus); one San Francisco (ex-State) Belt RR at Ft. Mason (now disused); one WP in San Francisco (now closed); and one Santa Fe in Richmond. In addition, there are two tunnels along the old right-of-way of the long-gone South Pacific Coast RR, between Los Gatos and Santa Cruz — one is now used for a records storage area. Tunnels have always been a big problem. In steam days, smoke would choke the

The Castro Point Railway's collection of antiques — all in working order.

Steam and car rebuilding shops (antiques and miniatures only)

Castro Point Ry., foot of Richmond Bridge, Richmond; California Ry. Museum, Rio Vista; Maker RR Shops, 2041 E. 14th St., Oakland; Redwood Valley Shops, 1399 Middle Harbor Rd., Oakland.

Tunnels, railroad

There are seventeen right around San Francisco: four on the SP in San Fran-

engineers. Now there are often rockslides, especially in tunnels that have wooden supports. Therefore, many have been closed, bypassed, or opened.

Turntables

Nine are in use: SP roundhouses, one each in San Jose and Brisbane; Billy Jones Wildcat RR in Los Gatos; four for cable cars in San Francisco; the Santa Fe roundhouse in Richmond; and a compressed, air-driven "floating" table for BART in Hayward.

Restaurants

In increasing numbers, these are feeding patrons' appetite for railroad nostalgia as well as for food. I have listed only those places that have come to my attention, here, and I welcome the chance to learn about any others I may have overlooked.

Oakland:

Spaghetti Depot, 3rd and Washington, is a former terminal of WP's "California Zephyr."

Pacifica:

Vallemar Station (1900), 2125 Coast

SP's old Berkeley Station, now a restaurant, with some local freight passing by.

Reconditioned stations and depots

Berkeley:

China Station, 700 University, is the old SP Berkeley station and is a tribute to the hundreds of Chinese workers who built the transcontinental railway.

The Depot, 1310 University. is a rather bizarre example of 1903 "Moorish" architecture. Converted to a restaurant in 1970, it was Berkeley's Santa Fe Station for nearly seventy years.

Calistoga:

Depot Cafe, 1458 Lincoln, may be the oldest depot-restaurant in California. Dating from 1868, it was part of the Napa Valley RR, later SP. Inside the cavernous warehouse is a reconditioned ceremonial car that reportedly was used in the Golden Spike celebration.

Livermore:

Old Livermore Ry., 25 N. "L" St., serves up meals in the old SP railroad station there.

Hwy. 1, is a living relic of the Ocean Shore RR.

Sacramento:

Western Pacific Depot Restaurant, 19th and J, was also a stop for the "California Zephyr."

Silver Palace Eating Stand is part and parcel of the Central Pacific Passenger Station in Old Sacramento.

Santa Cruz:

Old Santa Cruz Railway (1893) occupies the old SP depot at 123 Washington St.

Walnut Creek:

Walnut Creek RR Station and Dining Car, 850 Broadway, occupies the old SP station (1891) and the private car of Philip M. Africa.

Other Restaurants for Railfans

Not located in refurbished stations but aimed toward rail buffs are the Santa Fe Cafe, 1716 Divisadero, San Francisco, and the Whistle Stop Restaurant, Vintage Vinyard, Yountville. Located in an old commuter car since 1917 is San Francisco's Grubstake Restaurant, 1525 Pine.

Also not located in stations but in remodeled boxcars instead, are the fanciful Victoria Station restaurants. Aside from good food, they offer the American railfan an unusual feature — literally hundreds of relics and memorabilia of British Railways. They can be found at the Embarcaderos of San Francisco and Oakland, and in Sacramento, Sunnyvale, and Greenbrae (Marin County).

Similar in aspect, but not so faithful to railroaders is Cordelia Junction in Cordelia, at the highway junction of I-80 and I-680 (not a rail junction).

Pubs

Two pubs in San Francisco are devoted to (among other things) antique model trains. Henry Africa's, Van Ness at Vallejo, sports a display, and two models are constantly rattling along on a double track, stretching some 120 feet around the bar. The Boarding House bar, 960 Bush, features a history of trains, with dozens of handmade models on three walls. A Sacramento pub, the Whistle Stop in the Railroad Exchange Building, 1115 Embarcadero, features Old Sacramento railroadiana.

Railroad Museums — Live (for Riding) and Retired (for Admiring) Engines

Cable Car Museum, San Francisco

To call this historic building at Washington and Mason Streets in San Francisco a "museum" is insufficient. It is also the shops, car barn, and operating powerhouse for the cable cars. A portion of the gallery overlook area is devoted to the history and technology of the cable cars. The rest of the building is quite alive with activity. 42″ gauge.

San Francisco Cable Car Museum, 1201 Mason St., San Francisco, CA 94133, (415) 474-1887.

Equipment:

Live: Thirty-nine San Francisco cable cars (1886-1907); 0-4-0 gasoline "pusher" engine.

On exhibit: #8 Clay St. car (very small); #46 Sutter St. dummy (the "engine" that pulled a trailer); #54 trailer.

Schedule: Museum open daily 10-6, year-round; cable cars daily 7 A.M. til midnight.

Fares: Museum free, cable cars 25¢.

Also: Bookshop, shops, turntable, open cable driving wheels (sheaves).

California Railway Museum, Rio Vista Junction

This huge museum is located between Rio Vista and Fairfield on State Highway 12, and features sixty-eight pieces, including streetcars, interurbans, some steamers, and rolling stock. There is also a one-and-a-half-mile ride on electric equipment, and a complete trains bookstore. Standard gauge.

California Railway Museum-Bay Area Electric RR Assn., Rio Vista Junction, Solano County, CA 94571, (707) 374-2978.

Equipment: († denotes operable or serviceable)

Street and Suburban Cars (thirteen): Saskatoon Municipal Ry. #12 (1913)†; Pacific Gas and Electric #35 (1914); Sacramento Northern #62 (1920)†; S.F. Muni #178 (1923)†; Indiana RR #202 (1926)†; Key System #271 (1901); S.F. Muni #317 (1895)†; Key #352; Market St. Ry. #578 (1895) California-type†; Blackpool, England, Open Boat Tram #601 (1934)†; Key #987 (1927)†; S.F. Muni #1003 (1939)†; San Diego Elec. Ry. #1043 (1908).

Interurban and Elevated Cars (fifteen): Central California Traction #7 (1929) express car†; Peninsular Ry. (San Jose-Los Gatos) #52 (1903)†; Peninsular Ry. #61 (1903); Petaluma & Santa Rosa #63 (1905)†; Cedar Rapids and Iowa City #111 (1931)†; Key #182 (1937) articulated two-car†; Key #186 (1937) last car over Bay Bridge; SP (Interurban Electric Ry.) #332 (1911); Salt Lake and Ogden #400 (1910) trailer†; Salt Lake and Utah RR #751 (1913) observation trailer†; Interborough NY (IRT) #844 (1887)†; IRT #889 (1887)†; Sacto. North. #1005 (1912) passenger-baggage†; S.N. #1019 (1914) trailer†; S.N. #1020 (1914) trailer†.

Electric Locomotives (three): Cordelia Comet #2, 0-4-0 (oldest electric loco in Ca.); S.N. #652 (1928) steeple cab; S.N. #654 (1931) steeple cab†; Key #1001 (1910) steeple cab.

Diesel Locomotives (two): Cen. Cal. Traction #30, 0-4-4-0, seventy-ton (1947)†; Visalia Electric #502, forty-four-ton (1945)†.

Service and Work Cars (seven): S.F. Muni #C-1, yard switcher; S.F. Muni #0109 (1912) rail grinder†; S.F. Muni #1031 (pre-1907) crane car†; S.F.-Oakland Transit #1001 (1905) wrecking tool car†; Key #1201 (1896) line car†; Key #1215 (1899) shop switcher†; Key #1218 (1897) tower flat line car†.

Coaches (two): WP (Feather River) #653 (1913) lounge†; Circumnavigators Club Car, Pullman†.

Cable Cars (two): Market St. Ry. #22 (1907); Sutter St. Ry. #33 (1883).

Steam Locomotives (two): Pacific Coast #11, three-truck Lima Shay (1929)†; WP #334, 2-8-2 Alco (Schenectady) Mikado.

Rolling stock (twenty plus): Numerous boxcars, tankers, flatcars, cabooses.

Schedule: Weekends and holidays, noon-5 P.M., all year.

Fare: $1.50/75¢ (3-15 years), museum free.

Also: Museum, bookshop, RR shops, picnic area, refreshments.

Castro Point Railway, Richmond

This fine little railway is at Point Molate, Richmond. Follow signs to Point Molate Beach. Parked on an open hillside near the Richmond-San Rafael Bridge are several restored nineteenth- and twentieth-century engines in perfect working order. Nearby are shops where the restoration of older engines is in progress. The first Sunday of each month there are free rides, courtesy of the Pacific Locomotive Association. The three miles of the C.P. Rwy. are at the tail end of the Richmond Beltline RR Standard gauge.

Castro Point Ry., Pacific Locomotive Association, P.O. Box 2465, San Leandro, CA 94577.

Equipment:

Alive and/or well: #2, 2-6-2T American (1924); #3, 0-4-0 Porter (1913); #5, three-truck Heisler (1924); #12, three-truck Lima Shay (1903), ex-Sierra RR, the world's oldest Shay; #102, forty-four-ton GE diesel (1943).

On display and/or restoration: #4, 2-6-6-2 Baldwin Mallet (1924), ex-Clover Valley RR; #233, 2-6-2T Central Pacific Sacramento Works (1882), oldest local loco; #30, 2-6-2 Baldwin Prairie (1922), ex-Sierra RR; #101, ten-ton 0-4-0 Whitcomb diesel switcher (1925); #103 ten-ton 0-4-0 Plymouth diesel switcher (1929); #M-200 Skagit (1927) "Skunk" diesel rail car, ex-Cal. Western; gravity car, ex-Mill Valley and Mt. Tamalpais Rwy. (1896).

Rolling Stock: Three coaches (ex-WP, SP, and El Paso and SW'n), two passenger flatcars, one baggage car (ex-Yosemite Valley), one caboose (ex-NW Pac.), three freight flatcars, three refrigerator cars, one boxcar, two tankcars, a steam crane

Schedule: First Sunday of each month, 10-4, year-round; and July 4th.

Fare: Ride all you want for free.

Also: Beach with picnic area, refreshments, shops.

This geared Heisler engine, an uncommon lumber workhouse, is located at the Castro Point Railway.

Central Pacific Passenger Station, Sacramento

The State of California Parks and Recreation Department and the Railway & Locomotive Historical Society teamed up to give us this detailed reconstruction of the CP Depot in Old Sacramento at the Embarcadero. There are beautiful examples of antique locomotives and rolling stock, as well as a little cafe. In 1980, a huge museum next door with much more equipment (which now is in storage and restoration) will open with some forty railroad exhibits.

When this place was dedicated in 1975, there was a magnificent celebration. Old #12 herself — belching her smoke, hissing her steam, shrieking her whistle, and clanging her bell — broke the ribbon, while bands played, people yelled and cheered, a nearby Amtrak engine honked, and a passing SP freight blasted its whistle. It was enough to bring tears. But if you think that's something, just wait for the museum opening! Standard — and soon, narrow gauge.

Arcade Station, Central Pacific RR, Front St., Old Sacramento; or State of California Dept. of Parks and Recreation, P.O. Box 2390, Sacramento, CA 95811, (916) 442-8633.

Equipment, all but one retired, but very presentable:

Locomotives: Virginia & Truckee #12, "Genoa" (masquerading as Central Pacific #60, "Jupiter") 4-4-0 Baldwin (1873), occasionally on steam for special occasions; V&T #13, "Empire," 2-6-0 Baldwin (1873); V&T #21, "J.W. Bowker," 2-4-0 Baldwin (1875); Northwestern Pacific #112, 4-6-0 Baldwin Ten-wheeler (1908); in storage for display soon, SP #4294, 4-8+8-2 cab-forward Baldwin Mallet (1944).

Schedule: Open all year.

Fare: 50¢ (over 18 years).

Also: Restaurant, Sacramento Station of SP and Amtrak (a landmark), a statue to Theodore D. Judah (see p. 12), restorations in SP Unit (crane) shops nearby.

A dress-up pageant recreates the old times at the Central Pacific Station in Sacramento.

Harrison Street Railroad Park, Oakland

Right downtown in Oakland, this park sports one of the largest Baldwins on display in the Bay Area, a 4-6-0 Ten-wheeler, ex-SP. What's more, this big engine may be climbed on. Also on display are baggage and passenger cars from the early 1900s (ex-WP and Santa Fe) and a track inspector's pedicycle.

Roaring Camp & Big Trees Narrow Gauge Railroad, Felton

At the lower end of the Peninsula at Felton, off State Highway 9 near Santa Cruz, is a fine steam railroad. There is a beautiful five-mile ride in redwoods behind one of five magnificent steamers. The road features a switchback, built to substitute for a fantastic spiral trestle, under reconstruction after a disastrous forest fire in 1977. Thirty-six-inch gauge.

RC&BTNGRR, Felton, CA 95018, (408) 335-4484.

Equipment:

Locomotives on steam: "Dixiana," RC&BTNGRR #1, two-truck Lima Shay (1912); Big Trees Flume and Lumber Company #2, "Tuolumne," two-truck Heisler (1899); RC&BTNGRR #3, "Kahuku," 0-4-2T Baldwin (1890); RC&BTNGRR #4, "Waipahu," 0-6-2T Baldwin (1897); RC&BTNGRR #5, "Bloomsburg," two-truck Climax (1928) (the last one built). Also in use or storage are two diesel locos and three railcars.

Rolling Stock: Twelve passenger gondolas (1875-1896) (most ex-NCO), caboose, eight various freight cars (1870-1915).

Schedule: June-Sept., 11-4 daily; Apr., May, Sept., Oct., noon-4 on weekends and holidays, noon only Mon.-Fri.; Nov.-Feb., noon-3 weekends and holidays, noon only, Mon.-Fri.; June-Oct., Sat., 7 and 11 P.M. specials.

Fare: $5.00/3.00 (3-15 years).

Also: Bookstore, RR shops, picnic area, pioneer items, chuckwagon Bar-B-Q.

Railfan and Model Clubs, Supplies, and Bookstores*

Berkeley

Golden Gate Live Steamers, led by John M. Haines, has model facilities alongside the Redwood Valley Ry. in Tilden Park.

University of California, map room. Has maps from the beginning of railroads to the present.

Concord

Iron Horse Hobbies, 3529 Clayton Rd.

Emeryville

East Bay Model Club, 4075 Halleck St. Meets Sundays; public viewing of extensive indoor layout, third Fri. P.M.

Felton

Roaring Camp Bookstore. A good selection of rail lore.

Redwood City

Railway & Locomotive Historical Society, Pacific Coast Chapter, Fred Stindt, Chairman, 978 Emerald Hill Rd. Meets in the Clift Hotel, San Francisco every fourth Fri.

Rio Vista

Bay Area Electric RR Association, Hwy. 12. Supports California Railway Museum and organizes excursions.

California Railway Museum Bookshop, Hwy. 12, Rio Vista Junction. Probably the most complete railfan bookshop around.

Sacramento

Allgier's Train Repairs & Sales, 4095 Las Pasas Way. Gill's Train Shop, 2828 Marconi St.

Hammon's Archives and Artifacts, 1115 The Embarcadero.

Scale Trains, 1631 Arden Way.

Tracks 'N Trains, 24th at Fruitridge Road.

*If your favorite railroad club or model shop that specializes in railroads is missing from this list, you will be doing me a favor by letting me know. Hopefully, your entry will be included in our next edition.

This bell tolls for you in Felton at the Roaring Camp and Big Trees Railroad.

San Francisco

Bay Area Electric RR Association, P.O. Box 3694, S.F. 94119. Same as for Rio Vista association.

Bill's Terminal Trainatorium, 2253 Market St.

Bonanza Inn Book Shop, 650 Market St. — a good selection of railroad books.

Chan's Trains and Kits, Hyde at Jackson.

Golden Gate Model RR Club, J.D. Randall Junior Museum, 199 Museum Way.

Hobby Company of San Francisco, 5150 Geary Blvd.

Mailways (models), Folsom at Main.

Pacific Locomotive Association, 54 Hancock St. Supports the Castro Point Ry., organizes excursions.

Railroad Enthusiasts, Inc., Golden Gate Division, 1821 Pacific Ave.

San Francisco Public Library, Civic Center. Best selection of older books and historical information.

San Jose

Bill's Train Station, 2045 Woodard Road.

The Train Shop, 1611 Westwood Dr.

Western Railroad Society, Central Coast Chapter, P.O. Box 8407.

Whistle Stop, 1149 S. Saratoga-Sunnyvale Rd.

San Mateo

Northern California RR Club, P.O. Box 668. Meets once a month on 23rd and Mission Streets, San Francisco.

San Mateo Model RR Club, San Mateo County Fairgrounds.

Western Railroader, 235 E. Third Ave., P.O. Box 668, San Mateo, 94410. Francis A. Guido, publisher.

San Raphael

North Coast Model RR Club.

Sunnyvale

Engine House Electric Trains, 672 Alberta Ave.

Walnut Creek

Diablo Valley Model RR Club.

Whitman's Hobby Center, 1512 Locust Road.

Carmel

Thinker Toys, Carmel Plaza.

Santa Cruz

Manny's Toys & Trains, 1658C Soquel Dr.

Remnants of Early Railroads Around the Bay Area

The perfect roadbed of the Mill Valley & Mt. Tamalpais Scenic Ry. (1896-1930 — RIP) still exists from Mill Valley and Muir Woods to the summit. Now it is a hiking-biking path and fire road. A station platform survives about a mile east of Mountain Home. The Castro Point Ry. is restoring an old gravity car of this road, to be pulled by an old steam loco.

The bus station, in downtown Mill Valley, was the "Union Station" for the Northwestern Pacific and the Mt. Tam Ry. — both standard gauge, incidentally.

Several stations of the Ocean Shore RR are still extant, though they are now used as residences and commercial establishments.

The lower deck of the Bay Bridge and the East Bay Terminal (SF) are sites of the Interurban Electric Ry. (SP) and the Key System, which served the East Bay from 1939-1958. The sheds remain at the east end of the bridge by the toll plaza. Some cars of these lines and the Sac-ramento Northern, which also used the bridge, are on display at the California Railway Museum.

The Northwestern Pacific RR ferry docks in Tiburon are now used only by fishermen and seagulls; the roadbed in Tiburon is now a bike path; and the remaining tracks in the North Bay are now part of SP. A fully restored station is at Duncan Mills, on the now long-defunct Guerneville Branch.

In Point Reyes Station (Marin County), the North Pacific Coast RR (narrow gauge) station is now a community center. The old roadbed is clearest as it shortcuts marshes all along the eastern shore of Tomales Bay.

The Sacramento Northern used to run from Oakland to Sacramento as an interurban line; BART now occupies the western portion from Concord to Walnut Creek. Another portion, from Port Chicago to the long-abandoned ferry site near Pittsburg, is still used. Interruban cars still run at the California Railway

The Northwestern Pacific docks in Tiburon.

Museum, and the WP has some engines with the SN logo — why, I don't know.

Port Chicago, near Martinez, no longer exists, due to explosion danger from the nearby ammo dumps. Remnants are the SP and AT&SF stations, which are soon to disappear. Alongside are decaying tracks of the SN. Will this ex-interurban route someday be revived as the BART line to Antioch?

The only vestiges of the Ferries & Cliff House RR are the oft washed-out but still walkable roadbed from Seacliff, around Land's End, to Merrie (above the Cliff House), and the well-preserved Powell Street RR Station at 7th Avenue and Fulton Street in Golden Gate Park. This old steam line (1886-1906) ran from a cable turntable at Presidio and California Streets, out California to and around Lincoln Park, with a branch line over to the park.

A few feet seaward of the Dutch windmill in Golden Gate Park is an old brick bridge and the well-kept roadbed of the Park and Ocean RR (1883-1916) — a steam, later an electric, line. This line carried sightseers from Haight Street, along the park on Lincoln Way to the Great Highway, and from there to Fulton Street.

Some of the natives in Pacific Grove remember that, until a few years ago, the SP ran a slow freight engine out to a sand pit near Asilomar. But now the tracks from downtown Monterey to Pacific Grove are disused, and the new occupants of the old 1915 SP station in Monterey hear talk of removing the tracks completely. If the Del Monte Express is revived, one wonders where the line will terminate. Incidentally, along the line by Cannery Row (of Steinbeck fame) sits the hulk of Pickering Lumber Company #1, a standard gauge, three-truck Shay, decaying in piles of trash.

Much of the roadbed of the South Pacific Coast RR (1878-1887) as narrow gauge, then standard as part of SP), from Los Gatos to Santa Cruz is in fair condition. A tunnel of that line is now used to protect the storage of various records. There's some talk of reviving the line.

Many miles of the Petaluma & Santa Rosa RR (ex-interurban) are *still in use*, now as a branch line of the SP. The tracks pass right through the middle of Sebastopol's main street, on the way to an apple shed. As I looked at the California Railway Museum's beautifully restored P&SR car, I watched it pass, in my mind's eye, down the street.

Central California and the Sierra Nevada (South of Interstate 80)

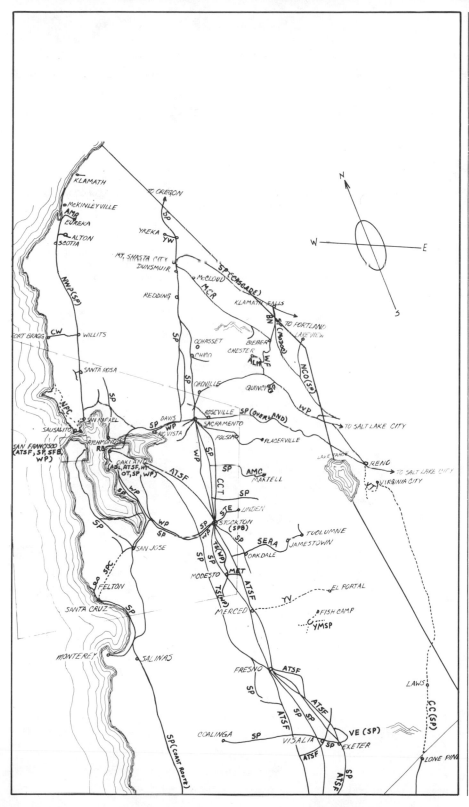

The vastly varied geography of the Central Valley and the neighboring foothills and mountains of the Sierra Nevada offer a multiplicity of types of railroading.

In the flat, irrigated agricultural regions, the railroads prosper, hauling hundreds of thousands of tons of produce annually. In the mountains, however, only the Amador Central, the Sierra, and the Camino, Placerville, & Lake Tahoe Railroads continue to serve the lumbering industry. The others have passed on.

A fortunate few have been revived, in part, to give us passenger excursions through the forests or mining camps. Here's what you will find in the foothills and in the Sierra from Tahoe to Yosemite Valley.

ABL	Alameda Belt Line
ALM	Almanor
AMC	Amador Central
AMR	Arcata & Mad River
ATSF	Atchison, Topeka & Santa Fe
BN	Burlington Northern
CC	Carson & Colorado
CCT	Central California Traction
CW	California Western
HT	Howard Terminal
MCR	Mc Cloud River
MET	Modesto & Empire Traction
NCO	Nevada, California & Oregon
NPC	North Pacific Coast
NWP	Northwestern Pacific
OT	Oakland Terminal
QR	Quincy
RB	Richmond Beltline
SERA	Sierra
SFB	San Francisco Belt
SP	Southern Pacific
SPB	Stockton Port Belt
SPC	South Pacific Coast
STE	Stockton Terminal & Eastern
TS	Tidewater Southern
VE	Visalia Electric
VT	Virginia & Truckee
WP	Western Pacific
YMSP	Yosemite Mountain—Sugar Pine
YV	Yosemite Valley
YW	Yreka Western
-----	roadbeds of extinct RRs

Rail Rides, Standard and Narrow Gauges

Amtrak

The Central Valley has its own special train: Amtrak's "San Joaquin," with brand-new equipment, is one of the most popular rides in California, judging from the public's response. There's one Amfleet train daily from San Francisco-Oakland to Bakersfield over Santa Fe tracks, with seven stops in between, costing only $21.50/10.75 (2-11) maximum one way, and only $24.50 round trip — if you return within three days.

The "San Francisco Zephyr" also runs this way — to Truckee and Reno, over a beautiful route. There are occasional winter ski excursions, with dancing aboard!

Sierra Railroad Company, Jamestown-Tuolumne and Oakdale, Tuolumne County

If you've ever watched railroad scenes on TV or the movies, it's a safe bet you've seen the Sierra RR. "My Little Chickadee," "High Noon," "Petticoat Junction," and some 100 other film productions continue to be made on this incredibly versatile line — so many, in fact that at times the regular freight service must be held up to accommodate film shooting schedules. Other freights in other, earlier times may also have been held up for shootings — but that's another matter.

Engine No. 28 of the Sierra Railroad built in 1922 — one of two used regularly.

Engine No. 3 historic steam locomotive of the Sierra Railroad was built in 1891.

Sonora, near Jamestown, was peculiar. A large number of its working population didn't want a railroad back in 1897. But they got one anyway, courtesy of the lumbering and mining interests. The SRR's fortunes went up in the 1920's, with lumber and hydroelectric projects. The Hetch-Hetchy RR, for one, was built to service the construction of the Hetch-Hetchy Dam in Yosemite Park, and was an offshoot of the SRR. The HHRR[1] lasted only until 1938, a time when the SRR was having big financial troubles, too.

But the line struggled, and survived, and now, as well as being the foremost railroad movie location in California, it is also doing a good local freight and passenger excursion business. Passenger excursions only go up the line to Standard, beyond there, the tracks and grass vie for supremacy into Tuolumne. But who knows? One day they may be used again for access to the new Westside & Cherry Valley RR (see p. 104) spread at the old West Side Lumber Company in Tuolumne.

Since its founding in 1897, the SRR, on Highways 120 and 49, has remained independent. It stars big Baldwin locos of the 1920s, dinner specials, two-three-hour rides, and a huge museum/roundhouse with turntable (Standard gauge).

[1]One remaining HHRR engine is on display at the Yosemite Valley RR Museum at El Portal (see p. 32).

Sierra Railroad Company, Drawer 515, Jamestown, CA 95327, (415) 983-3023, (209) 984-5388.

Equipment:

Live locos, steam: #3, 4-6-0 Rogers (1891), serviceable storage; #28, 2-8-0 Baldwin Consolidation (1922); #34, 2-8-2 Baldwin Mikado (1925).

Live locos, diesel: (local freight service and helpers for steam) #40, #42, #44 Baldwin-Lima-Hamilton (1955, 1955, 1951).

Rolling stock: Fourteen passenger cars (ex-SP); one observation car (1906); one mountain observation car (ex-Can. Pac.); one combination baggage-passenger car (ex-Cen. Cal Traction); three cabooses.

Schedules: "Cannonball," two-four a day, Sat. and Sun., Apr.-Oct.; two-four a day, Thurs. and Fri., June 23-Sept. 1; "Twilight Limited," Sat. P.M., July-Aug.; "Supper Special," Sat. P.M., Apr.-Nov.; "Wine & Cheese," "Beer & Pretzels," "Midnight," and other specials are also available (call for free brochure).

Fares: "Cannonball," $3.00/1.50 (5-15 years), under 5 free. "Twilight Ltd.," $13.75/3.85 (to 12 years), dinner, reservations. "Supper Special," $16.95, dinner reservations. Other specials, $9.00-$25.00.

Also: Roundhouse tours ($1.25/.60), refreshments, picnic grounds, museum (free).

Sierra Railroad's steam trains are always a treat.

Old Engine No. 36 of the Sierra Railroad emerging from retirement to work again.

Short Line Enterprises, Inc., Jamestown

Although it isn't part of the Sierra RR, this company has a good bit of equipment in working order for use in movies and TV productions. Stored and used on the Sierra line, it can be seen around the Sierra yards or "on location." Standard gauge.

Short Line Enterprises, Sierra RR Company, Stan Garner, Representative, 909 S. First Ave., Arcadia, CA 91006, (213) 681-5604.

Equipment:

Locomotives: #8, 4-4-0 Cooke American (1888) ex-Dardanelle & Russelville (Arkansas); #1, 0-4-0 Porter (1891); #99, 0-4-0 gas mechanical Davenport (1919); Railcar, Edwards (1926) ex-Bay Line ex-Tucson, Cornelia, & Gila Bend (Arizona).

Rolling stock: #3, coach ex-V&T; #8, coach combine ex-V&T; #12, baggage-mail car; #13, coach combine; #14, coach; #17 coach ex-V&T; #21, baggage car ex-V&T; three flatcars ex-V&T; refrigerator, gondola, boxcar, and caboose.

Other locos and rolling stock are under restoration.

The Virginia and Truckee Railroad is shown here once more under steam after a twenty-five year break.

Virginia & Truckee Railroad, Virginia City-Reno, Nevada

Although this elegant railroad made it to the Truckee River in Reno, it never made it to California, despite a plan to run it along that river in California. I am including it in this guide, however, because it's pretty close to California; because at least a part of it is running again under steam, after a hiatus of nearly twenty-five years; and because I suspect that California railfans will all want to sample it.

Virginia City, the home of the famous Comstock Lode, is perched 1,600 feet above the Carson River, only ten miles away. In 1869, this rich town needed a railroad to transport its thousands of miners, thousands of pieces of mining machinery, and thousands of gold bricks. The idea was to join Virginia City with Carson City and the Central Pacific in Reno. By 1872 the deed was done.

The Virginia & Truckee RR's first years were prosperous and fabulous. For years, it served as the connecting link between the Central Pacific and the Carson & Colorado RR (see p. 124), and was supported for several of those years by traffic from the latter. But the C&C was acquired by the SP in 1900, and it soon bypassed the V&T. The V&T struggled on its own through the ups and downs of mining until 1938, when the Virginia City section was abandoned. Its southern route into the agricultural districts of the Carson River kept it alive until 1950, when its last train ran.

Now, the only standard-gauge steam in Nevada is running again — and this time you can ride it. The twenty-five-minute ride is three miles long, passing several mine workings to a tunnel, which is being cleared. Although the V&T is old, the present-day operation is quite new, and it needs much public support. Thus far, the owners are using temporary equipment until they can obtain their own.

Bob Gray, Pres., Virginia & Truckee RR Company, Virginia City, NV 89440, (702) 847-0380.

Equipment: (as of this writing; this equipment is subject to change)

Locomotive: #29, 2-8-0 Baldwin (1916).

Rolling stock: #25, #26 original coaches, #54 gondola, #50 caboose, #54 excursion car.

Note: Much of the V&T's remaining original equipment is scattered, but a remarkable amount is nearby in various hands.

In Virginia City: Engine #27, 4-6-0 Baldwin Ten-wheeler (1913); bullion car #13.

In Carson City (Nevada State RR Museum State Park): Engine #25, 4-6-0 Baldwin Ten-wheeler (1905), several cars. To be on hand, late 1978: #18, "Dayton," 4-4-0 Central Pacific (1874); #22, "Inyo," 4-4-0 Baldwin (1875), both on loan to the National Park Service in Utah. Also in Carson City, caboose #24.

In Sacramento (Central Pacific Station, p. 91): Engines #12, "Genoa," 4-4-0 Baldwin (1873); #13, "Empire," 2-6-0 Baldwin (1873); #21, "J.W. Bowker," 2-4-0 Baldwin (1975).

Schedule: Memorial Day-Sept., daily; Sat., moonlight; Oct. and Thanksgiving, weekends, as weather permits.

Fares: $1.85/1.00 (5-21 years); all-day pass, $5; group rate 75¢/student.

Also: The attractions of historic Virginia City, bookshop.

Virginia City, Nevada, the home grounds of the Virginia and Truckee Railroad.

Westside & Cherry Valley Railroad, Tuolumne, Tuolumne County

It takes a lot of tacos to buy a railroad, but one guy who had both the desire and the tortillas was Glen "Taco" Bell. Along with the railroad, Bell got the former headquarters and mill of the West Side Flume and Lumber Company.

And now the railriding public has a beautiful, 340-acre park in which to sample one of the best narrow-gauge logging railroads in the Sierra. Bell operates the Westside & Cherry Valley RR as an "operating museum," devoting several portions of the park to representations of former eras of California history.

WS&CVRR covers five miles of the former lumber company's lines into the woods, uses their old sheds, reclaims their buildings, and has converted the mill pond to a swan pond.

With the Sierra RR so near, we now have the advantage of two kinds of rails to be enjoyed in one area.

Westside & Cherry Valley Ry., Tuolumne, CA 95379, (209) 928-4282.

Equipment: 36″ gauge, 5+7½ miles track.

Locos, steam: #12, "George W. Burgess," three-truck Lima Shay (1927); #15, three-truck Lima Shay (1913).

Locos, in restoration: #2, two-truck Heisler (Stearns) (1899); #7, three-truck Lima Shay (1911).

Locos, on display: #7 and #33, three-truck Shays, ex-Sugar Pine Lumber Company, both standard gauge, along with several standard gauge freight and passenger cars, made up in trains.

Locos, diesel: 0-4-0 Plymouth switcher (c. 1939), also several gasoline "speeders" (railcars); 1939 Pontiac auto with steel wheels, ancient Caterpillar switcher.

Locos, gasoline: ancient railbus for weekday rail transport.

Rolling stock: Some forty passenger gondolas, flatcars, workcars, and cabooses, some for riding, others for display.

Schedule: Winter months, weekends only, 11-6. Spring and summer schedules not available at this writing. Please contact WS&CV for these.

Fares: Steam, $3.00/2.00; railbus, $1-3.00/1-2.00 (3-12 years), depending on length of ride.

Also: Spacious picnic grounds, antique working-auto displays, various period exhibits, ponds and boats.

Yosemite Mountain-Sugar Pine Railroad, Fish Camp, Madera County

The tracks on a 1920s map of the Madera Sugar Pine Lumber Company logging railroads have the look of a huge root system. When the MSP's predecessor laid its first tracks in 1889, the area adjacent to Yosemite National Park was heavily forested and nearly impenetrable. The easiest way to extract this wooden bonanza was with a narrow-gauge railroad network.

Tracks were laid down, the timber was removed, and the tracks were then removed to another part of the forest. Until it became a victim of the Depression in 1931, the MSP had spread out 140-mile tentacles of track. Today, a forest service map of that portion of the Stanislaus National Forest shows those same roadbeds as backwoods service roads and trails. It is a strange experience to drive one of those two-rut roads and suddenly find yourself in a deep railroad cut within the forest's interior.

Into this setting came the Yosemite Mountain-Sugar Pine Railroad in 1967, as a pet project of its owner, Rudy Stauffer. The YMSP was laid on an old MSP roadbed and uses a magnificent 1932 Shay loco, late of the Pickering and then the West Side Lumber Companies. The forest has regrown now, and the train of open flatcars with log benches hisses down a 4-percent grade to a glen on Slab Creek, where a watering stop is made. The train slowly chuffs back up — and at the end of the ride, you have gone four miles and experienced a real logging-road site. At the end, there is abundant "railroad" activity of switching, recoupling, and huff-puffing about. On board, the tour is expertly guided. The Shay is the largest narrow-gauge engine of its type ever built.

Yosemite Mountain-Sugar Pine RR, Fish Camp, CA 93623, (209) 683-7273.

Equipment: 36'' gauge, two miles of track.

> **Locomotives:** #10, three-truck Lima Shay (1928); #5, ten-ton gas-mechanical Vulcan; #10, railcar, Ford Model A.

> **Rolling stock:** Three passenger gondolas (ex-log cars), tank car, side dump car.

Schedule: May 1-mid-June, and Labor Day-Oct. Steam on weekends, railcar weekdays; mid-June-Labor Day, steam daily except Mon. and Fri., railcar Mon. and Fri. (steam 10:30-3:30, railcar 9-4); late Sat. night specials with BBQ and entertainment.

Fare: $3.60/1.80 steam; $2.80/1.40 (4-12 years) railcar; Sat. Special $4.50/2.25.

Also: Logging museum, bookshop, picnic area.

Rail Rides, Miniatures

Folsom Valley Railroad's "Nevada," once known in Berkeley as the "Cricket."

Camino

During the apple and pear harvesting season (October and November), the El Dorado, Boa Vista, & Apple Ridge Railroad, operates weekends at the Boa Vista Orchards, Apple Hill Rd. The quarter-mile road uses a 4-4-0 nineteenth-century-style gasoline Onan, about thirty years old. Fare and tour is 60¢, and caters to school groups as well as to the general public. Nineteen half-inch gauge, three inch scale. Phone (916) 622-5522.

Idlewild Park, Reno

Located alongside the Truckee River, there are rides on a gasoline-powered streamliner, J.C.T1. Fare for the trip around a large pond is 25¢. Operations are June 1-Labor Day, Tues.-Sun., noon-8 P.M. (702) 785-2000.

Folsom Valley Railroad, Folsom

Twelve-inch gauge, three-inch scale. The smallest of the miniature gauges, the "Nevada" is a creation of Erich Thomsen, and was once in Tilden Park, Berkeley, under the name "Cricket." It has hauled nearly a million passengers! The design dates from the first trains that ran from Sacramento to Folsom. The ride through Folsom City Park is seven minutes and is adjacent to a first-class zoo. The coal-fired steam locomotive is #1, "Nevada," 4-4-0 Ottaway-Thomsen, American-style (1950), and pulls eight cars, including passenger gondolas, cattle car, and caboose. The schedule is 12-5 weekends and holidays, Jan. 15-Nov. 15, weather permitting. Fares are 50¢. Twelve-inch gauge, 4" scale.

Pixie Woods, Stockton, on Mt. Diablo Ave.

There are rides on #9, 2-4-0 Arrow Development Corporation, 1880s-style engine, about a 4″ scale, 20″ gauge. The ride runs through a well-manicured park with a lagoon off the Stockton Channel, and over a nice bridge. It costs 30¢. The schedule is 12-6 P.M. daily in summer, and only on weekends during winter. (209) 466-9890.

Roeding Park, Fresno

This park features the Roeding Park Railroad, a 20″-gauge, 3″ scale almost-replica of #118, "C.P. Huntington," a 4-2-4 Chance train of 1974 vintage. A portion of the line is triple rail to obviate the necessity for a switch on the loop. The quarter-mile ride is a bargain 10¢. It runs daily from mid-Mar. to mid-Oct. (10-5), and on weekends the rest of the year. The owner is the Fresno Rotary Club; access from Belmont Exit, off Hwy. 99. (209) 233-3980.

Operating Freight Roads and Their Shops/Yards

Three Major Roads in Three Locations

Historically, *Stockton* was the first major railroad junction city in California. It is located at the crossroads of Central California's east-west and north-south lines. The multitude of tracks to be crossed and negotiated right in the middle of the main streets attest to its continuing importance as a railroad city, with three major and three short lines serving the city, the port, and the environs.

Only the Santa Fe passes through without much ado — that is, its yard and transfer facilities are minimal, since it has a big yard in Richmond.

The Southern Pacific maintains service yards and a transfer point for the large exchange traffic with the AT&SF and the WP.

The Western Pacific gave a boost to Stockton when it consolidated all its shops and repair facilities in that city in 1969. At the shops, alongside Airport Road on the south side of town, one can observe an impressive amount of round-the-clock activity. The old roundhouse is still very much in use, as is its turntable.

In the adjacent yards, trains are made up for their transcontinental journey, and every afternoon a train departs for Modesto on the now-absorbed Tidewater Southern route. Doing local switching are half a dozen diesel antiques of 1930s vintage, some equipped with grotesque spark arresters, reminiscent of nineteenth-century diamond stacks on steamers.

On my last visit, I learned that the WP was having some trouble keeping its newly hired women on switching duty, owing to some nineteenth-century notions of one or two yardmasters. The Santa Fe and the SP have already begun to overcome this problem; let's hope the WP will do so soon.

Elsewhere in the Central Valley, the other large railroad center is *Bakersfield*, for two reasons. At the southern extremity of the valley, Bakersfield is the collecting and distributing point for trains arriving and departing for Los Angeles and the southern transcontinental routes.

Also, all rail traffic southbound from Bakersfield must funnel through the one line (SP) out of the valley, over the 3,800-foot Tehachapi Summit (see p. 119). For this gigantic task, both the AT&SF and the SP provide booster engines for the numerous trains at their spacious yards in Bakersfield. Standing on the overpass spanning the SP yards, one can't help but be awed at the steady parade of trains over this essential stretch of track.

There is one important Nevada city in this area that benefits the California railroading public — *Reno*. It was once the junction of the Central Pacific, the Nevada, California, & Oregon, and the Virginia & Truckee railroads. Now, the two remaining roads have been transformed into the SP and the WP.

The WP occupies the NCO's Line into Reno, and the SP's yards in Sparks exist mainly as a division point for transcontinental trains, and to cut in and out helpers using the gruelling 7,000-foot-high Donner Summit route. Some snow removal and maintenance equipment is also kept ready there.

Short Lines

Now for the short lines. As everywhere, they cover the spectrum from flourish to flop. As examples of the latter, consider the fates of the Pacific Coast Ry. and the Yosemite Valley RR, described in Part I (see p. 30 and p. 32).

The standard-gauge short lines, located in agricultural regions, which have ceased as independents, at least have not suffered the indignity of having their rails ripped out. Traffic was still profitable, so the major roads simply integrated them into their networks. Not so the logging roads. When the timber disappeared, so did the rails.

In this section, I have taken the liberty of extending the geographical "Central" region westward to include the agricultural districts of Santa Barbara and Ventura Counties, which are more akin in nature to the Central Valley than to Southern California.

Amador Central Railroad, Martell-Ione, Amador County

The Amador Central is one road that still prospers from the lumbering industry — these days, it has some new track, and an engine is being refurbished. Its owner, the American Forest Products Company, maintains it as a common carrier, as well.

Once it had steamers, as the mouldering turntable in Martell reveals; but now it manages on two diesels. The AMC was founded in 1908 as the Ione & Eastern Railroad, but in 1918 it took its new name, and in 1945 it went diesel.

Adjacent to the old station-depot is the Martell Inn, a landmark of the region and the residence of several lumber company employees — a good bar for chatting in.

Amador Central RR, Martell, CA 95642, (209) 223-1660

Equipment: Standard gauge, eight miles mainline.

Locos: #9, 120-ton Baldwin (1951); #10, 120-ton Baldwin (1952).

Rolling stock: Two ballast cars, one flatcar.

On display (in Ione): #7, 2-8-2 Baldwin (1901).

Also: Nearby in Jackson, the Amador County Museum and old gold mine diggings, shafts.

Nathaniel Hawthorne (1804-1864):
"House of Seven Gables" (1851)
"Railroads . . . are positively the greatest blessing that the ages have wrought out for us. They give us wings; they annihilate the toil and dust of pilgrimage; they spiritualize travel!"

Camino, Placerville & Lake Tahoe Railroad, Pollock Pines-Placerville, El Dorado County

Above Placerville lies a fifteen-mile railroad along a route that almost became the first transcontinental railroad. During the big struggle to become first, Placerville interests lost out to the Central Pacific route. After the initial flurry, the town even had trouble getting the CP to put a line that far in 1883.

Nevertheless, the lumber industry later saw to it that Theodore Judah's original route got some tracks laid upon it — in the form of the CP&LT. The railroad initially was a project of the American River Land & Lumber Company of 1890, and was brought as standard gauge from Placerville to the finishing mill in Pollock Pines. As the name implies, Judah's route was surveyed all the way to Lake Tahoe, and the parent company, the Michigan-California Lumber Company still owns title to it. But timber had to be hauled out on narrow gauge, and that took precedence over yet another transcontinental route.

In one of the most unusual engineering feats of California railroading, the CP&LT narrow-gauge trains (cars, not usually engines) passed to the company sawmill over the 1,200 foot deep American River canyon on a cable that was 2,650 feet long! The system lasted until 1949, when a fire destroyed one of the supports.

Steam excursions on a narrow-gauge portion continued until recently. One of the locomotives sits in perfect shape on a pedestal, going nowhere until insurance rates go down.

Camino, Placerville, & Lake Tahoe RR, Michigan-California Lumber Company, Camino, CA 95709, (916) 644-2311.

Equipment: 36″ and standard gauges.

Locos, steam: #1, "Little Cecil," 0-4-0T Porter (1899) ex-West Side Lumber Company and Hetch-Hetchy RR, serviceable storage.

Locos, on display: #2, two-truck Lima Shay (1884), one of only three Shays with vertical "haystack" boiler; #11, a tiny 0-4-0T Vulcan (Schenectady) switcher (1900-01).

Locos, diesel: #102, double-ender GE (1941).

Rolling stock: Fifty leased boxcars, pea green.

Modesto & Empire Traction Company, Modesto-Empire, Stanislaus County

Few who keep up with the railroad world would dispute the statement that the Modesto & Empire Traction Company is the state's most rapidly expanding rail enterprise. The M&ET began around the turn of the century as a tiny interurban connection — only five miles long — between the SP in Modesto and the AT&SF in Empire. In 1909, it was bought by T.K. Beard, the son of an early Stanislaus County pioneer.

Things went along modestly until the Beard family began a new industrial complex in the late 1940s, alongside the M&ET east of the city of Modesto. By constructing and leasing a great number of warehouses, packing sheds, and factory facilities, all well served by tracks of the M&ET, the railroad and its parent, the Beard Industrial District, found themselves doing business in a style that made the big lines big.

When I visited the district, I found everyone *very* busy, in an efficient office adjacent to an immaculate roundhouse. It's the way to run a railroad.

Modesto & Empire Traction Company, 11th St. at F, Modesto, CA 95354, (209) 524-4631.

Equipment: Standard gauge, five miles mainline.

Locos: #600 (1949), #601 (1949), #603 (1955), #604 (1954); #606 (1955), #735 (1946), ex-Tidewater Southern, now in Cannibal. All GE.

Rolling stock: One flatcar.

Central California Traction Company, Stockton-Sacramento, San Joaquin and Sacramento Counties

Founded in 1907, primarily as an interurban transit line from Stockton to Sacramento, the CCT saw its passenger business dwindle. (Where didn't passenger business dwindle?) But unlike some other lines, the CCT managed to change its emphasis and went into a strictly freight business, non-electric.

The change didn't keep this Jonah, however, from being swallowed by three joint whales: The Santa Fe-WP-SP. This arrangement provides for joint ownership by the three giants, but operation, with big red engines, is independent. (You can usually figure that if a road has its own engines, its operation is an independent one.)

The CCT's four road-switcher engines poke along the fifty miles through fertile fields at no better than twenty-five m.p.h., collecting and distributing the produce of the many farms and agricultural businesses along the way. At night, the engines sleep in the same old redwood frame and tin-roofed building in which the rapid interurbans were put up so many years ago.

Central California Traction Company, 1645 E. Cherokee, Stockton, CA 95202, (209) 466-6927.

Equipment: Standard gauge, fifty miles mainline.

Locos: #42, 100-ton Alco (1940s); #60 and #70, GM-EMDs; #80, Alco (ex-Tidewater Southern).

Rolling stock: Three cabooses, one flatcar, one boxcar.

(Note: Several older pieces of CCT equipment are still extant in museums. See index.)

Santa Maria Valley Railroad, Santa Maria-Guadalupe, Santa Barbara County

As far back as 1877, the SP built a line near (but not to), Central City, in a slowly developing agricultural valley along the windy, foggy central coast. But Central City, later to become Santa Maria, didn't mind much — it had the narrow-gauge Pacific Coast RR.

The problem arose, though, of trans-shipping produce from one gauge-type car to another; and the citizens of Santa Maria decided that the solution was a standard-gauge connection to the SP. Thus was born the Santa Maria Valley Railroad.

Later, the PCR disappeared, and oil wells up the valley appeared, as did a lot of agriculture. Now, the SMVRR is thoroughly ensconced as a local institution. The road even uses some of the old PCR roadbed in Santa Maria.

Santa Maria Valley RR, Jones St. at McClelland, Santa Maria, CA 93454, (805) 922-7941.

Equipment: Standard gauge, twenty-nine miles of track.

Locos: Eight GE diesels, #10, 20, 30, 40, 50, 60, 70, and 80 (1949-1956).

Rolling stock: Three bright yellow cabooses.

(Note: There are two old steamers of the SMVRR around, #205, 2-6-2 Baldwin Prairie (1920s) (Santa Maria Fairgrounds); #21, 2-8-2 Baldwin Mikado is still in existence somewhere.

Stockton Port Belt Railroad, Stockton

This is a trackage road only, owned by the city of Stockton, but operated with yearly rotation by WP, SP, and AT&SF.

> *Edward Morgan Forster (1879-1970):*
> *"Howards End" (1910)*
>   *"Railway termini are our gates to*
> *the glorious and the unknown.*
> *Through them we pass out into*
> *adventure and sunshine, to them, alas!*
> *we return. . . ."*

Stockton Terminal & Eastern Railroad, Stockton-Linden

Shortly after 1900, a group of San Joaquin County farmers, merchants, and, alas, rascally promoters joined to put together a railroad eastward from Stockton. Their thousands of stockholders came from all walks of life, even sailors — making this a rather uncommon thing, a railroad not owned by big capital. Through several fits and starts, they succeeded in laying down a track in 1910, and immediately began incredible bickering and an internal war.

The California Railroad Commission and a commission to regulate investments were constantly harping at the road to straighten out its finances. But the only engine got ditched in the mud, and by 1917 the ST&E was in receivership. Just as other roads struggled with mines or pines, the ST&E wrestled with agricultural fortunes.

It also scuffled with city hall, and it never made it to the Stockton Terminal. Business on the eastern end shriveled, as did the track. Somehow it survived the Depression, probably only because everyone had to eat — and agricultural products were the life of the ST&E.

Slowly, then more rapidly, better management brought better business. A remarkable transformation occurred with the directorship of the Beard family, who used a technique that had breathed life into the Modesto & Empire Traction Company. New warehouses, sheds, and tracks were constructed in a manner that would make the old, big lines envious.

Olive Davis, in her biography of the ST&E[1], gives that line pet nicknames, which reflect its history over the years: "Stop, Talk, & Eat" (early infatuation); "Stop Talking & Eat" (things are tougher); "Slow, Tired, & Easy" (things are really rough); "Strong, Tenacious, & Energetic" (recovery); "Swift Transport & Excursion" (fantasy, courtesy of the admen).

(Note: There are occasional excursions to the Linden Cherry Festival; there is a new roundhouse; and there are new offices.)

Equipment: Standard gauge, thirty-six miles of track (ten miles mainline).

Locos, diesel: #505, 506, 507, 100-ton Alcos (1942); #557, 560, 564 Alcos (1940s).

Locos, steam: #3, 2-6-2 Baldwin Prairie (1922), in rebuilding.

Rolling stock: Two private cars, four passenger cars, one diner, one caboose (ex-YV).

(Note: Engine #1 is at Travel Town, Los Angeles. See p. 140) Stockton Terminal & Eastern RR, 800 N. Shaw Rd., Stockton, CA 95205, (209) 948-4803.

---

[1] Olive Davis, *The Slow, Tired, & Easy RR* (Fresno: Valley Publishers, 1976).

Sunset Railway, Gosford Feed Lot-Taft, Kern County

Before the days of pipelines, rails carried the oil. Around 1890, oil was discovered in the lower-west corner of the Central Valley, and two railroads were built to carry it away to Bakersfield.

Around 1892, the McKittrick Railroad was carried to that town and its "sister" line, the Sunset Railway, was carried to Taft. The former is now a branch line of the SP; the latter fell to two owners, the SP and the AT&SF, which alternate operation every five years.

The Sunset does a fair business with a slow train, hauling in pipe and oil tanks for the always-drilling oil companies every other day. The return trains carry propane, onions, and kitty litter. (Bet you never would have guessed where that came from. Or do you care?)

In Taft, the old yellow depot is now an antique store. The tracks move out across the desert of greasewood and metal refuse of the oil fields, the blue sky pierced by a scattering of ancient derricks that have withstood the elements for three-quarters of a century.

Ventura County Railway Company, Oxnard-Port Hueneme

Oxnard was one of those several places in California that the big SP bypassed in its hurry elsewhere. In 1906, the citizens of Ventura County, wanting to develop their port and lacking SP support, built their own railroad to it.

Today's business is varied, local, and naval (the Port Hueneme Naval Station is at the end-of-track). Some of its twenty miles of track are hidden behind tall rows of blooming oleander, giving the VCR a rural look, although it's in the midst of a growing city.

Locomotives: #1, seventy-ton GE (1948); #4, seventy-ton GE (1946).

Ventura County Railway Company, 250 E. 5th St., Oxnard, CA 93030, (805) 483-5214.

Visalia Electric Railroad, Exeter, Tulare County

This is one of those railroads that has been totally assimilated by a giant — in this case, the SP. There's not much left but the tracks, which are to be found at the wye (a "Y"-shaped junction) in Exeter. The Exeter Chamber of Commerce building nearby is not the old station; it just looks like it. Some of the old electrical equipment is in fine working order at the California Railway Museum.

Local Railroadiana

Steamers on display

There are a surprising number of old steam locomotives to be seen in this area. Most have been donated by the railroads to mark the history of those engines that made California railroads famous. Some of them are still running.

Angels Camp. See Angels Camp Museum.

Bakersfield. See Kern County Museum and Pioneer Village.

Camino-Pollock Pines. See Camino, Placerville, & Lake Tahoe RR.

Carson City, Nevada. See Nevada Historical Museum and Nevada State Railroad Museum.

Coulterville, Hwy. 49 intersection. Here you'll find an 1800's 0-4-0 mine engine, the like of which is not displayed in California.

El Portal. See Yosemite Transport Museum, pp. 32, 116.

Fish Camp. See Yosemite Mountain Sugar Pine RR ("Rail Rides").

Fresno, Roeding Park. SP #1238, 0-6-0 Baldwin switcher (1918) and a "40 & 8" French boxcar.

Ione, downtown, adjacent Bank of America. Amador Central #7, 2-8-2 Baldwin Columbia (1901).

Jamestown. See Sierra RR and Short Line Enterprises ("Rail Rides").

Modesto, Modesto Children's Park. AT&SF #2921, 4-8-4 Baldwin Mohawk (1944), a real giant.

Placerville, Downtown Exit on Hwy. 50. SP #1771, 2-6-0 Baldwin Mogul that saw service on the branch line that snakes up into the hills west of town.

Santa Maria, Santa Barbara County Fairgrounds. Santa Maria Valley RR #205, 2-6-2 Baldwin Prairie (1920s) — in sad shape.

Stockton, Pixie Woods Park. SP #1251, 0-6-0 Baldwin switcher (1918) — a victim of vandals.

Tuolumne. See Westside & Cherry Valley RR ("Rail Rides").

Virginia City, Nevada, old Virginia & Truckee Depot. V&T #27, 4-6-0 Baldwin Ten-wheeler (1913). Also see Virginia & Truckee RR ("Rail Rides").

Restaurants

Jamestown, "Railtown, 1897," at the Sierra RR Depot, located in a streamliner dining car.

Oakdale, "Red Caboose Restaurant," Hwy. 120, west of town.

Tahoe City, "Victoria Station," 425 N. Lake Blvd.

Visalia, "The Depot," an elegant restaurant, Oak and Church Sts., located in the old, Spanish-design SP depot.

"Just Jenny," an old-timer that worked as a logging engine and now rests at Angels Camp.

Museums

Angels Camp, Angels Camp Museum, on Hwy. 49. Features "Just Jenny," 2-2-0 Lane Owen Dyer (Ill.) Dolbeer-type logging engine (1876). Also other steam logging equipment and mining relics.

Bakersfield, Kern County Museum and Pioneer Village, Chester Ave. On display, SP #2914, 4-8-0 Schenectady (1898); AT&SF caboose; Carson & Colorado (SP) narrow-gauge boxcar; Bena Station (brought here). Also on the grounds is a curious eight-foot square structure with laminated wooden walls six inches thick. The SP used it on flatcars while building new track. It's the SP jail!

Carson City, Nevada, Nevada Historical Museum and nearby, Nevada State Railroad Museum. NHM: Inside, Virginia & Truckee engine models; outside, Lake Tahoe Railway & Transportation Company #1, 2-6-0 Baldwin (1875). The LTR&T road ran from Truckee to Tahoe City (Ca.) as an excursion line from 1900 to 1943. Engine #1 is three-foot gauge, but the tracks were standard from 1926. NSRM: In a germinal state of assembly and construction along Hwy. 50, south of town. Locomotives: V&T #25, 4-6-0 Baldwin Ten-wheeler (1905) in restoration; V&T #18, "Dayton," 4-4-0 Central Pacific (1874) and #22, "Inyo," 4-4-0 Baldwin (1875) are due in from Promontory Point, Utah, once the museum is open. Rolling stock: Several work cars, wooden coaches, and a French "40 & 8" boxcar.

El Portal, Yosemite Transport Museum. A not-too-kempt collection of items, including Hetch-Hetchy RR #6, three-truck Shay (ex-Pickering Lumber Company), an old station, and an old White bus. Under National Park Service direction.

Jamestown, Railtown, 1897. Part of the Sierra RR's large outlay of early equipment. See Sierra RR ("Rail Rides").

Tuolumne, Westside & Cherry Valley RR. Several working logging engines run among a variety of "theme" historical areas. See WS&CVRR ("Rail Rides").

Model Shops

Bakersfield

Friesen Model Trains, 1702 Julian.

Fresno

Tom's Trains, 2245 E. Hammond Ave.

Stockton

Pardini's Toys, 1177 W. Hamner Lane.

South Lake Tahoe

Bob's Hobbies & Toys, 1014 Al Tahoe Blvd.

Southern California--
The Desert and Owens Valley

The one characteristic common to the railroads of the Mojave Desert is that, except for those that simply pass through here on their way to somewhere else, they all originally sprang from mining.

On these lonesome stretches, there aren't many railroads to ride out here. In fact, there are only two.

ATSF	Atchison, Topeka & Santa Fe
CC	Carson & Colorado
CO	Calico & Odessa
DV	Death Valley
EMT	Eagle Mountain
HI	Holtville Interurban
LAH	Los Angeles Harbor
LAJ	Los Angeles Junction
PCR	Pacific Coast
SBC	Sonora-Baja California
SDAE	San Diego & Arizona Eastern
SMV	Santa Maria Valley
SP	Southern Pacific
SUN	Sunset
TR	Trona
TS	Tidewater Southern
TT	Tonopah & Tidewater
UP	Union Pacific
USG	Union States Gypsum
VCY	Ventura County
VE	Visalia Electric
----	roadbeds of exticnt RRs

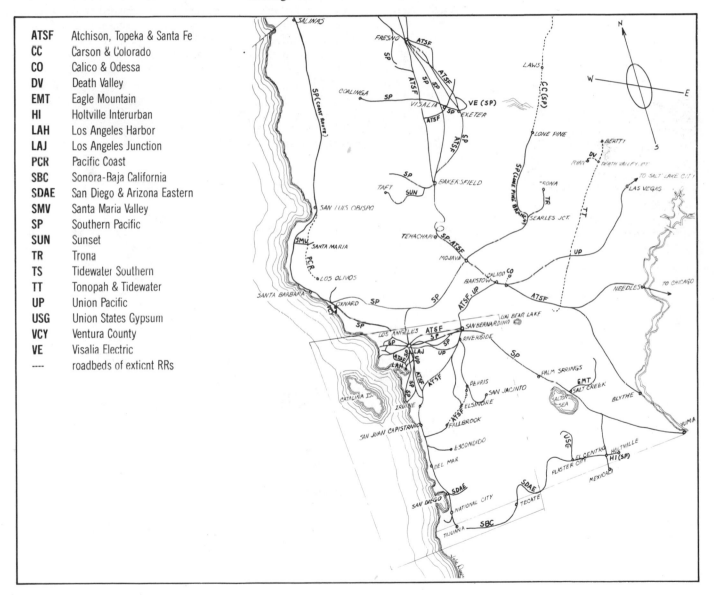

Rail Rides

Amtrak

Amtrak does a good job of covering the state — even the desert region. Even though you may travel 120 or 170 miles between stops, there are still stations in Needles, Barstow, Yuma, and Indio. But that's it; and all those stops are made in the dead of night. It isn't a particularly fascinating way to see the desert, is it?

Try the next entry.

Calico & Odessa Railroad, Calico, San Bernardino County

In 1881, back up in the dry hills east of Barstow, a great silver deposit was found. To carry the crude ore to a large crushing (stamp) mill near the SP (later AT&SF) tracks at Daggett, the Oro Grande Mining Company built a 30''-gauge track for its two tiny 0-6-0T locos and mining cars in 1888. On and off until 1903, depending on the fluctuating fortunes of mining, the Calico Railroad operated. Then the town of Calico became a ghost.

But in 1950, Walter Knott (of the Berry Farm — see p. 129) began reviving the townsite into one of the few tourist attractions of that part of the Mojave Desert. Knott, well known for his interest in rails, rebuilt a section of the old railroad, dubbing it the Calico & Odessa Railroad, after the town and an adjacent canyon.

Today's C&O has a single engine, constructed as an approximately half-scale replica of the original. At first it was steam-powered, but lack of water forced its conversion to gasoline power. The cars are passenger-adapted original ore cars. The road runs about half a mile around the tailings and ruins of the desolate mining camp.

To convey visitors from the parking lot to the high mesa, a cable car was installed in 1951 at the site of an earlier mine tramway, using 1907-vintage ore cars that originally were used on the Calico RR.

Shafe-Malcolm Enterprises, Barstow, CA 92311, (714) 254-2252.

Equipment: 30'' gauge, c. 6'' scale.
  Loco: #5, 0-4-2T G.M. Lovsted Company (1958).
  Rolling stock: Four covered gondolas (old mine cars).
  Cable tram: Built at Calico (1951), design of old mine trams; open gondolas are restored ore cars (1907).
Schedule: 364 days, 8-6 P.M. (Closed Christmas.)
Fares: C&ORR: .75/.35 (4-16 years). Tram: .50/.25.
Also: Adjacent to the station are the original mine tracks and cars, as well as many features of the "restored" ghost town.

Operating Freight Roads and Their Shops/Yards

Three Major Lines in Two Locations

Most trains, having attained the high desert, highball it out of there. After all, there's no reason to stop, except for an occasional mine or the yards in Barstow. Consequently, in that immense expanse of land, only two towns are rail centers — *Mojave* and *Barstow*.

Mojave

Mojave is the junction of the AT&SF and the SP, on their common way to the Tehachapi Summit from Barstow and San Fernando, respectively. In addition, it is the station where both roads add and subtract their helpers for that summit. Mojave is also the junction of SP's Lone Pine Branch, the remnant of the former trans-Sierra route through the Owens Valley (see p. 124). Today, its principal business is lumber and soda ash.

Barstow

I arrived in Barstow at 2 A.M. one summer night and, surprising a preoccupied Amtrak ticket agent, inquired about the strange Moorish building in which he was sitting. "It's the ol' 'arvey 'ouse," he replied grumpily. A large sign on the railroad platform reading "Casa del Desierto" added nothing to his cryptic explanation. Well, the next day I found out that it's the old Fred Harvey House, once a bustling desert inn run by the famous chain that served many a meal to railriders. Now it is deserted.

In 1975, the Santa Fe installed a magnificent marshalling yard to make up its trains bound for the east and for Los Angeles and the Central Valley. Some hands say it's already too small, but it looks impressive, and I'm sure it speeds up operations. Nearby are the Santa Fe's shops that service hundreds of engines — all the major work on the entire railroad. I'm told that Barstow was chosen for both these operations because land is pretty cheap here.

Around the area are a derrick and a flanger (although there's not much snow in these parts), and an unusual two-car track-inspection vehicle (#9166).

The Union Pacific also passes by here, having shared some track with the Santa Fe coming up Cajon Pass from San Bernardino; but a few miles out, it splits for Las Vegas and Salt Lake City.

The Tehachapi Loop

How do you get a railroad from 500 feet to 3,800 feet in only thirty miles with a severe restriction on the grade? In 1876, William Hood, SP's construction engineer solved that problem by making the tracks into a loop, resembling the first steps of a scout's bowline knot, followed by eight tunnels.

This spectacular feat, the Tehachapi Loop, is a state historical landmark, and as such is marked on Highway 58 at Keene, directing passersby to a vista point overlooking the loop.

The day I stood at the overlook, a very long SP train appeared with four smoke-belching engines at the head and no less than six helpers toward the end. The slow parade snaked up the loop with a roaring hum that reverberated off the dry canyon walls — surely the most awesome demonstration of a railroad's tremendous power to be felt anywhere in California.

Desert Short Lines

In spite of the erratic demand for some mining products, of availability of raw materials, and of vicious weather, four independent mining railroads are holding their own, and very well, too. One little ex-interurban lost its independence but not its tracks, and one long short line first lost its autonomy, and then, in a hurricane its tracks, as well — the Holton Interurban and the San Diego, Arizona, & Eastern. Happily, the SD&AE has since recovered both its independence and its tracks.

Eagle Mountain Railroad, Eagle Mountain-Salton Sea, Riverside County

Back in the Eagle Mountains lies a rich iron ore deposit. To feed the furnaces of Fontana, where oxide is made into steel, Kaiser Industries built a railroad in 1946. This fifty-two-mile road carries the ore from the mine to an SP junction on the Salton Sea, and over it pass 100 cars a day, each containing 100 tons of ore, five days a week.

The railroad uses four engines to haul every load over its 1½-percent grade. The mine is accessible by road, ten miles from Desert Center, off Interstate 10.

Kaiser Steel Corp., Eagle Mountain, CA 92241, (714) 392-4413.

Equipment: Standard gauge, fifty-two miles.

    Locos: Five GE diesels #1030-1034 (1968).

    Rolling stock: One dump car, one flatcar. The ore cars are leased from SP.

Mojave Northern Railroad, Victorville, San Bernardino County

The Sierra Nevada and the coast ranges of California are mainly granitic in nature, so limestone in the state is pretty scarce. Where good deposits exist, there is frequently a cement plant.

A large limestone quarrying and cement plant operation is to be found at the Southwestern Portland Cement Company at Leon, near Victorville. This company first constructed tracks to its mines in 1915, and has expanded them to a current total of eighteen miles. In actuality, the Mojave Northern RR exists as only the original portion of these tracks; the cement company owns and operates the rest.

Mojave Northern RR, Southwestern Portland Cement Company, P.O. Box 937; or North End E St., Victorville, CA 92392, (714) 245-1681.

Equipment: Standard gauge, eighteen miles.

    Engines: #408 (1948), #409 (1946), #410 (1952) — all 120T Fairbanks-Morse, bearing SWPCC decals.

    Rolling stock: Several bottom-dump new and old ore cars — about ten to a consist.

(Note: MNRR #2, a saddle-tank steamer, is now at the Orange Empire Railway Museum, Perris.)

Trona Railway Company, Trona-Searles Junction, San Bernardino County

Around 50,000 years ago, the desert of Inyo-San Bernardino Counties was wet. And Searles Lake and Death Valley were collecting the soluble salts of the runoff of thousands of acres on mineral-rich mountains. Then the rains ceased, the lakes dried up, and huge deposits of salts were left on the lake floors. Some of these salts now keep our collars clean. Others are put to use by dozens of industries, from medicine to photography.

In 1862, to transport the thousands of tons of chemicals to the Los Angeles market, teams of twenty or so mules were employed. But, this was very inconvenient, and a railroad was deemed far more suitable. Slowly, various railroads worked their way into the region; the SP's Lone Pine Branch was the closest.

Finally, in 1916, after four months of construction, the thirty-one miles of the Trona Railway Company connected to the SP with the mineral deposits of Searles Lake. As did most short lines in the Depression, the TRC discontinued passenger service in 1937; however, for six years it operated a railbus. In 1954, the line was completely dieselized, and even today two of their original Baldwins see service in the Trona yards.

I presume that this highly specialized line will continue for many years; the Kerr-McGee Chemical Company owner has just completed a large processing plant, Searles Lake has only barely been tapped, and demand for their chemicals is ever-expanding.

Trona Railway Company, Trona, CA 93562, (714) 372-4031.

Equipment: Standard gauge, thirty-one miles.

Locos: #52 Baldwin (1954); #51 Baldwin (1951), original equipment; two road units leased from SP.

Rolling stock: Several hopper cars and box cars, with "Trona Chemicals" and "KM" logos leased from SP.

Henry David Thoreau (1817-1862):
"Walden" (1854)
"We do not ride on the railroad;
it rides upon us."

United States Gypsum Company, Plaster City, Imperial County

A silver engine led ten silver cars down a very straight line in a white desert. The train appeared to be not so much a string of gypsum-loaded cars as a diminutive Amtrak. Out on the desolate but beautiful line, we rumbled past live, spent shells of the naval weapons station adjacent; we could have passed deer, coyotes, or a bighorn sheep, but not on this run.

The U.S. Gypsum Company likes its dusty little 3'-gauge trains to haul about eighty cars a day to replenish the rockpile stockpile. In 1976, the rockpile was all used up when the railroad was out for several weeks, following the disastrous flood that washed out the San Diego & Arizona Eastern RR (which serves the mill). Following the flood, the entire work force of the plant donated a day's work on the railroad to help restore this essential part of the mill to operation. Such is the dedication of the employees at Plaster City.

The railroad, constructed in the 1920s, is the one remaining industrial narrow gauge in California. And from all reports, it will be around for quite a while; demand for gypsum is waxing, and there is plenty more gypsum where the last fifty years' supply came from.

U.S. Gypsum Company, Plaster City, CA 92261, (714) 358-7721.

Equipment: 36'' gauge, twenty-six miles.

Locos: #1203, seventy-five-ton GE (1946); #1303, 1403, fifty-ton GEs (1956).

Rolling stock: Twenty silver rock cars, tamper, two speeders, one flatcar, and a watercar hauled each day to the waterless mine.

Railroadiana

Museums, Restaurants, Retired Steamers

Barstow, Barstow County Museum, Barstow Rd. Some items of interest to railfans. Open Mon.-Fri. only.

Barstow Station, 1611 E. Main St. A McDonald's in a railroad diner. Also has an eighteen-car complex of shops. On display, WP's private car, "Doris Duke."

Death Valley National Monument, Furnace Creek Ranch Museum. On display: Death Valley RR #2, 2-8-0 Baldwin Consolidation (1916), 3' gauge; "Baby Gauge" chain-driven gasoline engine, 24" gauge (rusting away); Koppel Industrial Car Company "mucking machine" mine engine (1922).

El Centro, Imperial Valley College. Old Holtville Depot is now an art gallery; buckboard on portion of desert plank road stands outside.

Imperial, Imperial County Fairgrounds. SP (SD&AE) #2353, 4-6-0 Baldwin Ten-wheeler (1912); Imperial Irrigation District #151, 0-4-0T Alco (Cooke) (1918), saw work on Colorado levee. Also passenger coach and county museum.

Independence, Dehy Park. On display: SP #18, 4-6-0 Baldwin (1911), 3' gauge from Carson & Colorado (SP).

Laws, Laws Railroad Museum and Carson & Colorado RR. See description following this listing.

Oro Grande, Griffith Henshaw Playground. On display: UP #2564, 2-8-2 Baldwin Mikado to play on.

Rosamond, Tropico Gold Mine. Mine railroad tracks and mine cars. Some SP buildings from Palmdale. Gold mine. Admission, $1.50/1.00 (5-11 years). Winter, weekends 10-4; summer, daily 10-4.

Just to show that fashions in trains change, too, Union Pacific's venerable No. 22, a wood-burning locomotive, is shown next to the streamliner "City of Los Angeles."

Laws Railroad Museum, Laws, Inyo County and the Carson & Colorado Railroad, Mound House, Virginia City, Nev.-Keeler, Lone Pine, Ca.

Begun as an idea to connect the Virginia & Truckee RR (see p. 102) with southwestern Nevada, the Carson & Colorado RR ended as an interstate railroad from Hazen, Nevada to Keeler, California. During its life it was lengthened, changed, shortened, widened, and nearly abandoned. The C&C did start, in 1880, as a three-foot narrow gauge at the V&T's Mound House station; and, as mining booms and local pressures demanded, it went some distance into Nevada. But when the original direction switched, it found itself servicing the communities and mines of the Owens Valley instead.

The old story of played-out mines and see-sawing silver prices just about brought it down by 1900. But in that year it was saved from an early death by none other than C.P. Huntington of the SP. The SP revived it, as did new mines in and around Tonopah, Nev. It even acquired a new name: the Nevada & California RR.

Yet, it stayed as a sore appendix, stretching a couple of hundred miles from the north into the Owens Valley until 1910, when the construction of the Los Angeles aqueduct access by the SP brought a standard-gauge line from Mojave up to its terminus at Owenyo.

Then it was possible to travel from Los Angeles, if one had a couple of transfers and plenty of time, to the Virginia City area. As often happened on sparsely used lines, truncating began. From 1932 until 1960, chunks of the line were put out of service. It was rumored that the eminent E.M. Frimbo rode the line late in 1945, after taking the "last steam" train of the Tonopah & Goldfield RR, a feeder line.

Finally, in April 1960, the last valiant little steam engine pulled into the Laws terminal from Owenyo, where it remains isolated to this day.

Northern parts of the line had been standard-gauged to Mina, Nevada as early as 1905, and the southern portion (as SP) was always standard gauge; so this little narrow-gauge orphan just wasn't suited to modern freight movement. It couldn't adapt, but it had served well for eighty years.

The northern portion is still there — passing the crumbling ruins of Ft. Churchill a few miles east of Carson City. That southern portion still sees a few trains a week to Lone Pine. When I visited the Lone Pine Station, I found no pine, only loneliness. There is a large railroad station — yellow paint peeling, nearly deserted — and a spreading desert with dry, towering mountains. A clump of boxcars and the glint of polished rails made it slightly less forlorn. Three-foot gauge.

Bishop Museum & Historical Society, P.O. Box 363, Bishop, CA 93514, (714) 873-5950.

Equipment on display:

Loco, steam: SP #9, 4-6-0 Baldwin (1909), retired only in 1960 — sister loco in Independence.

Loco, gasoline: "Blue Goose," Brill (1920), ex-Death Valley RR, in decrepit condition.

Rolling stock: Made up as a train — three boxcars, one gondola, one stockcar, one passenger-baggage combo.

Also on grounds: Turntable, water tank, other cars on blocks, depot museum.

Schedule: May-Nov., daily 7-4; Dec.-Apr., weekends 10-4.

Fare: Donation.

Also: Excellent bookstore, picnic grounds.

Remnants

The desert heals its scars only very slowly. Because of this, road-beds and relics of the many mining ventures that have succumbed may yet be found in most areas. In addition to the railroads and relics in local museums (see preceding pages), I have also described the fortunes and remains of three other railroad undertakings — the Epsom Salts RR (p. 31), the Tonopah & Tidewater (p. 19), and the Death Valley RR (p. 27). This is not, of course, an exhaustive list; and for the railfan who wishes to explore further, I recommend starting with David Myrick's book, *The Railroads of Nevada and Eastern California.*[1]

Edna St. Vincent Millay (1892-1950):
"Travel" (1921)
> *My heart is warm with the friends*
> *I make,*
> *And better friends I'll not be*
> *knowing;*
> *Yet there isn't a train I wouldn't*
> *take,*
> *No matter where it's going.*

---

[1] David Myrick, *Railroads of Nevada and Eastern California,* Vols. 1 and 2 (Berkeley: Howell-North, 1962).

Southern California--
Los Angeles and San Diego

Rail Rides, Standard and Narrow Gauges

There are five types of rides on larger equipment in the Los Angeles-San Diego region. As usual, we start with Amtrak, but we also have live steam, courtesy of the two Walters, Disney and Knott. Magic Mountain has a diesel, and the Orange Empire Railway Museum atmosphere is electric with different rail rides. Travel Town, awaiting some expensive trolley repairs, is not operating rides.

++++ Amtrak routes
1 Anheuser-Busch Monorail
2 Magic Mountain
3 Tropico Gold Mine
4 Universal Studios
5 Travel Town
6 Griffith Park & Southern RR
7 Union Station
8 Huntington Library
9 Museum of Science & Industry
10 Los Angeles Co. Fairgrounds
11 Knott's Berry Farm
12 Lomita RR Museum
13 Ford Ave. RR Drawbridge
14 Disneyland
15 Lion Country Safari
16 Orange Empire Ry. Museum
17 San Juan Capistrano Depot
18 San Diego Wild Animal Park
19 San Diego Co. Fairground
20 Old Town; ATSF Depot
21 Balboa Park

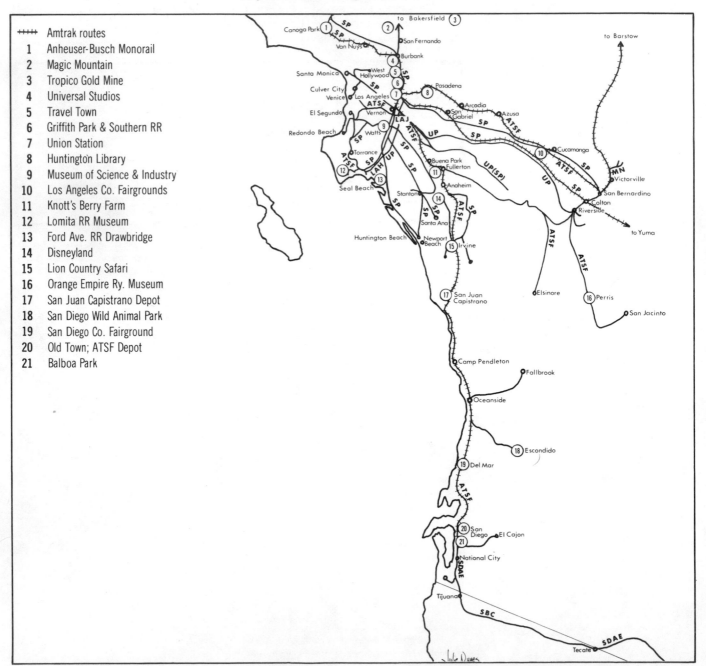

Amtrak's southbound "Coast Starlight," shown here leaving the California hill country and heading toward the ocean near San Luis Obispo en route from San Francisco to Los Angeles.

Amtrak

You can't take a daylight ride in extreme Northern or Southern California, but you can around here — even on just a sightseeing tour. I recommend the morning "Coast Starlight" to Santa Barbara, with an easy afternoon return. The round-trip fare is only $16. Or try any of six daily trains on the LA to SD run. Stop off at San Juan Capistrano, or San Clemente's beach. Sorry, but the "Sunset Limited" and the "Southwest Limited," L.A. to Pomona and/or Indio, don't have the best of daylight schedules.

It's getting to be a little like the good old days, with railroad excursions out to the countryside on weekends. As Amtrak says, "Train yourself to relax."

Disneyland, Anaheim

Something tells me that only a few railfans are going to go to Disneyland just to ride the trains. But while you're there, you might as well.

Walt Disney himself was a railfan from way back — he built a little steam miniature for his back yard, then had two engines built for Disneyland (others for Disney World in Florida), and rescued/restored two other antiques.

I am compelled to say that getting this information required penetrating layers of sticky park bureausecrecy, which required some boot cleaning afterwards.

The big trains are all steam; the rides are a long twenty minutes over one and a quarter miles of a loop around the park.

Disneyland, 1313 Harbor Blvd., Anaheim, CA 92803, (714) 533-4456; Engines maintained by Retlaw ("Walter" spelled backwards) Division, 1333 Flower St., Glendale, CA, (213) 245-0121.

Equipment: 36″ gauge, one and a quarter miles.

Locomotives: #1, "C.K. Holliday," 4-4-0 Disney American (1953); #2, "E.P. Ripley," 4-4-0 Disney American (1953); #3, "Fred Gurley," 2-4-4 Baldwin (year?), ex-Louisiana sugar plantation; #4, "Ernest S. Marsh," 2-4-0 Porter-type (year?), ex-mining 0-4-0T engine.

Rolling stock: Several trains, one of five long covered gondolas, one of seven short gondolas plus caboose, one of four gondolas and passenger car, each train holding 215-285 passengers. (They carry five and one-half million passengers per year.)

Schedule: Year-round, summer 8-1 A.M., winter 9-1 A.M.

Fares: Admission and some rides, from $8.50/5.50 (3-11 years); prices vary with type of ticket book purchased.

Also: About half a mile of horse-drawn streetcar ride; number, year of construction, and gauge not available. Casey Jr. Circus Train, miniature 1800s-style; details not available.

Monorail. See special section on "Monorails."

One of the four trains of the Disneyland Railroad prepares to depart the picturesque Main Street Station for a twenty minute circle tour of Disneyland.

Knott's Berry Farm, Buena Park

Knott's is indeed a good place to go ride on a number of old railroad relics. The steam equipment, kept in top operating condition, is from the Rio Grande Southern RR and the Denver & Rio Grande RR, two Colorado roads that later coalesced into the Denver & Rio Grande Western. The RGS and the D&RG were narrow gauge; the D&RGW was both narrow and standard.

Outside the grounds, around the parking lot, six San Francisco cable cars circulate. They have been converted to electric battery power, but they retain the grip and brake levers.

Knott's Berry Farm, 8039 Beach Blvd., Buena Park, CA 90620, (714) 827-1776.

Equipment: Steam, 36'' gauge, three-quarter-mile track.

Locos: RGS #41, 2-8-0 Baldwin (1881); D&RG #40, 2-8-0 Baldwin (1881); D&RG #464, "Mudhen," 2-8-2 Baldwin Mikado (1903).

Gasoline railbus: RGS #3, "Galloping Goose," Pierce-Arrow (1929).

Rolling stock: Eight passenger cars, ten passenger-carrying freight cars, all wooden, most from RGS and D&RG, earliest 1880.

Cable cars: California St. #6 (1906); #17 (1907); #20 (1907); #49 (1913); #59 (1914); Market St. Ry. #1, all 42'' gauge.

Also: Calico Mine RR, a short miniature ride, is also inside the grounds. There are five engines, 0-4-0T diesel-powered Hurlbut mine engine-style (1963), 14'' gauge, 3'' scale, along with twenty "mine cars" for passengers.

A railride of sorts is the *Corkscrew* rollercoaster that makes a 360° loop.

Outside the grounds is the Lagoon Train #1033, 4-4-4 1880s-style Hurlbut (1963), 14'' gauge, 3'' scale.

Schedule: Year-round, daily outside the grounds, inside closed Wed.-Thurs., Labor Day-Memorial Day.

Fares: Park admission $5.25/3.75 (3-11 years). Rides: train 60¢, mine 60¢, rollercoaster 85¢. Ticket books are also available. Outside: Lagoon Train, 40¢, cable cars 25¢.

Once upon a time this train wound around the deep canyons of Colorado country. It now rests at Knott's Berry Farm.

Magic Mountain, Valencia

There is more to be found at Magic Mountain than rail rides, but since rails are such a substantial part of the park, let me describe them one by one.

Magic Mountain, Magic Mountain Pkwy., Valencia, CA 91355, (805) 259-7272 or (213) 367-2203.

Railroads, diesel: The "Grand Centennial Excursion," a ride into the last century, is aboard some of the thirty-year-old narrow-gauge equipment of the Monolith Portland Cement Company of Tehachapi. There are two GE engines, twenty-five-tons (1948), and ten covered gondolas, ex-cement cars. Also on this line is the "John Bull," a whimsical approach to the original vertical boiler engine, built at Magic Mountain. It is powered by a Cummins hydraulic diesel (1975). Three-foot gauge.

Railroads, steam miniature: #99, 4-4-0 Crown Metal Products (1973), propane-fired, with five gondolas. The ride is a half-mile, eight-minute scenic loop. Twenty-four-inch gauge, three-inch scale.

Railroads, funicular: Rising 450 feet with two red cars, not unlike the defunct Angel's Flight, is the full-sized, three-foot gauge funicular line built in 1970 by the Kornenburg Shipbuilding Company in Austria.

"Metro" monorail: See following section in "Monorails."

Also on rails, but not railroads: "Mountain Express" roller coaster, "Bradley" roller coaster (for smaller kids), "Gold Rusher" roller coaster, and the six-story-high looper, "Revolution."

Schedule: Summer, daily (Memorial Day-1st week after Labor Day); winter, weekends and holidays (except Christmas), morning thru night (hours vary).

Fare: $9.50/7.50 (3-11 years) for unlimited use of all rides and attraction.

Orange Empire Railway Museum, Perris, Riverside County

Twenty years ago, electric transit in the Los Angeles area was on the verge of disappearing. In 1956, anticipating the ultimate passing of the nation's finest rail-transit system, a small, dedicated group of railfans founded the "Orange Empire Traction Company" to preserve what they could of that era.

The size of this group has multiplied to more than 800 members. Their holdings have expanded to more than 100 pieces, making it the largest rail museum in California. Even the name has metamorphosed, as steam, passenger, and freight rolling stock have been added to this living museum.

The tracks occupy a portion of what, in 1883, was the California Southern (AT&SF) San Bernardino-San Diego mainline — before rains prevailed over rails in the nearby Temecula Canyon.

Orange Empire Railway (formerly, Trolley) Museum, P.O. Box 548, Perris, CA 92370, (714) 657-2605.

Equipment: 42″ and standard gauges (*denotes body only; †denotes operable).

Street and Suburban Cars (thirty-five): Hill of Howth (Ireland) #2 (1901); Bakersfield & Kern #4 (1900); Los Angeles Ry. #7 (1895); Fresno Traction Company #51 (1913); FTC #83 (1925); LAR #151 (1898); LAR #152 (1898); S.F. Muni #162 (1914); S.F. Muni #171 (1923)†; Pacific Electric #179 (1912); PE #331 (1918)†; PE #332 (1918); San Diego Elec. Ry. #508 (1936); PE #511 (1901)*; LAR #525 (1906); PE #538 (1909); PE #637 (1922); LAR #665 (1911)†; PE #717 (1925)†; LAR #744 (1911)*; New Orleans Pub. Serv. #913 (1923); San Diego Elec. Ry. #1003 (1936)*; LAR #1160 (1923)†; LAR #1201 (1921); LAR #1423 (1924); LAR #1435 (1924); LAR #1350 (1924); LAR #1559 (1925); LAR #2501 (1925)*; LAR #2601 (1930); LAR #3001 (1937); LAR #3100 (1943)†; LA Transit #3165 (1948)†; PE #5123 (1922); PE #5166 (1925).

Interurban Cars (eleven): Bamberger Elec. RR #127 (1932)*; Key System #167 (1937)†; Visalia Electric #301 (1908)*; PE #314 (1930)†; PE #418 (1913)†; PE #498 (1913)†; PE #1000 (1913)*; PE #1001 (1913); PE #1045 (1908)*; PE #1046 (1908); British Columbia Elec. Ry. #1225 (1913).

Electric Locomotives (four): American Smelting & Refining Company #1 (1912); Hutchison & Northern (Kansas) #1 (1921)†; Sacramento Northern #653 (1928)†; PE #1624 (1924)†.

Service & Work Cars (M/W) (nine): PE #00150 wire greaser (1936); PE #00157 tower car (1915)†; PE #1440 (1910)*; LAR #9209 (1913); LAR #9225 five-ton derrick (1912)†; LAR #9310 rail grinder (1925)†; LAR #9350 tower car (1907)†; LAR #9351 line const. car (1907); LAR #9550 shop switcher (1904).

Funeral Streetcar (one): LAR "Descanso" (1909).

Coaches & Baggage Cars (sixteen): SP "Sacramento" private car (?); Kyoto Tramways #19 (1896?)†, 42″; Virginia & Truckee #20 combo (1885?); Cal. Southern Ry. Museum

#54 private car (1924?)†; AT&SF #60 Ry. P.O. (1930?); San Diego & Ariz. Eastern #175 combo (1915)†; UP #204 class car; Denver & Rio Grande Western #552 combo (1891); D&RGW #743 baggage (1910); AT&SF #2055 Ry. P.O./combo, †; UP #2065 Ry. P.O. (1914); AT&SF #2543 combo (1904?); AT&SF #2602 Ry. P.O. (1925)†; AT&SF #3010 chair car (1925?)†; AT&SF #198814 obs. (1910)†.

Steam Locomotives (two — in restoration for use): Mojave Northern #2, 0-6-0T Davenport (1917); Ventura Co. RR #2, 2-6-2 Alco Prairie (1923).

Gasoline and Diesel Locos (three): S. Cal. Edison #12, four-wheel gas-mech. switcher (1942)†; Trona Ry. #E-60, four-wheel, twenty-five-ton GE diesel (1948); Trona Ry. #E-513, four-wheel diesel-hyd. switcher (1956).

Other Rolling Stock (thirty-two plus): Nine cabooses, four flatcars, eight boxcars, two refrigerator cars, one stock car, two gondolas, one hopper, one wrecker tender, one foreman's car, one wheel car, two steam derricks (1912, 1915), three trolleybuses, one AT&SF horse express car (1930).

(Note: The OERM is constantly expanding its holdings. This list will be updated as new stock is reported.)

Schedule: Rides weekends and holidays (except Thanksgiving and Christmas) 11-5, grounds open 9 A.M., daily Christmas week to New Years and week before Easter.

Fares: $1.25/.75 (5-11 years); $2/$1 all-day pass. Three-quarter-mile loop and three-quarter-mile on old Cal. Southern R/W.

Also: Bookstore, picnic grounds, museum.

Rail Rides, Miniatures

Three of the parks listed in the previous section as featuring large-scale rides also provide rides on miniatures. See that section for some details on these miniatures.

Magic Mountain Steam Ride

Knott's Berry Farm, Lagoon Train

Disneyland, Casey Jr. Circus Train.

Griffith Park & Southern Railroad

Located in Griffith Park at Los Feliz, Los Angeles, has three trains: #104, a Superchief-style streamliner by the Railroad Supply Corp. (1975) with five cars; #1344, a UP-diesel style switcher by Keiller (1977) with four cars; and an SP Alco-style streamliner with three cars. The ride is one and a quarter miles long and is seven minutes (the best deal that miniatures have to offer). The GP&SRR has been in operation for thirty years. They are open 10-5 Tues.-Fri., and 10-6 weekends and holidays. Fares are 50¢/35¢. Eighteen and a half-inch gauge, three-inch scale. (213) 665-5188.

The Balboa Park Railroad

Right by the zoo in San Diego, is the city's only miniature. It is a half-mile ride of three minutes on 16″ gauge. The train consists of #501, Miniature Train Company GM F-3 diesel-type with four open cars holding sixty passengers. 35¢, 2½″ scale. (714) 239-4748.

Lion Country Safari

Located midway between Los Angeles and San Diego, near El Toro, has a steam miniature. Somehow this brightly-painted little train looks very appropriate, chugging amidst hippos, flamingos, and a savannah mud wallow. The engine, #99, 4-4-0 Crown Metal Products (1973) pulls four cars over a half-mile round trip. Three-foot scale, twenty-four-inch gauge. Park admission is $4.95/3.25 (3-11 years) and is open year round from 9 or 10 A.M. to 5 or 6 P.M., depending on the season (but to 3:30 P.M. in winter). (714) 837-1200 or (213) 485-8951.

Other miniature *steam* rides may be obtained (with permission of the owners) at the Sunday functions of the Los Angeles Live Steamers club in Griffith Park, L.A., and the Chula Vista Live Steamers group in Rohrer Park, Chula Vista.

This Lion Country steam engine chugs past hippos, rhinos, and flamingos.

Rail Rides, Monorails

The Los Angeles-San Diego area is fortunate in having five monorail-type operations. There are essentially two varieties of systems — the suspended and the mounted. The suspended type utilizes cars hung from an overhead rail, whereas the mounted type sits atop the rail, and may be more suited to use in trains. The California monorail systems are used to transport visitors within a small, scenic area, and not for rapid, mass movement of people.

Anheuser-Busch Brewery

16000 Roscoe Blvd. in Van Nuys. A suspended monorail is used for a tour of the brewery. It was constructed by the Arrow Development Company in 1966, has ten twenty-four-passenger cars on a three-quarter-mile track. The twelve-minute ride runs 1-6 daily, and is free.

Disneyland

Its monorail is perched on a concrete overhead rail. It moves rather rapidly, in trains of four cars each that were built by Alweg-Disney in 1959. The ride covers two and a half miles in ten minutes, but it's a bit rough — the "rail" is concrete; the wheels are rubber. Fare for the monorail only is $1.25.

Los Angeles County Fairgrounds

Passengers are carried in ten suspended cars built in 1962 by the American Crane & Hoist Company. The cars are the first of their kind in California. Operation is only from mid-Sept. to mid-Oct., during the Fair season.

Magic Mountain

People move around by means of the "Metro" monorail, which travels 3,400 feet. It was designed by the Habbegar Company of Tunn, Switzerland. This mounted-type monorail first saw service when the park opened in the mid-1970s.

Wild Animal Park in Escondido

For want of another word, an electric bus "monorail" — which describes the power and guiding system of this special train — runs in this park. The shop crews even speak of "bogeys," not "trucks," for the wheels, but the operator need not steer these huge, bus-size cars. The ride offers a spectacular five-mile, hour-long trip through the barren, rocky hills, amid the habitat of African, Asian, and South American wild animals — right at the trainside. There are six two-car trains operating at 480 volts, built by Rohrer (1972), as well as car #19, maintenance/wrecker with gasoline engine (1972). Admission to the park and all parts is $5.25/2.75 (6-15 years). It is open daily, Memorial Day weekend to Labor Day 9-9; and weekends, Sept. through Oct. 9-9; post Labor Day-Oct., weekdays 9-5; Nov.-Feb., 9-4; March to Memorial Day, 9-5. (714) 747-8702.

This is one of four trains in the world's first daily operating monorail system, the Disneyland Monorail System, speeding above the Submarine Lagoon in Tomorrowland.

Regional Freight Roads-- Their Shops/Yards

Major Roads, Los Angeles

Los Angeles has had a long history as a rail center — first, because of the agriculture in the L.A. basin; then, because of the subsequent steady growth of the population and industry; and finally, because of the increasingly busy harbor that followed that growth.

A strip southward from downtown L.A. is the district for most of the older yards — of the SP, the UP, and the AT&SF.

The SP's Taylor Yards and shops are fairly easily seen from the eastern slopes of Elysian Park, but they are difficult to observe closeup. The busy shops, at the Southern Division headquarters, maintain a big crane with a work train, and an often-used turntable, which is used to store engines in the narrow yards. Other SP yards are to be found in Industrial City. The main marshalling yards are in Colton, which is the departure point for transcontinental trains bound eastward to Texas and northward to the Central Valley and San Francisco.

Not far south of the Taylor yards, Amtrak has taken over and remodeled the old Santa Fe Ninth Street (coach repair) Yards for its own use, as well as the old Santa Fe roundhouse and turntable of the Redondo Yards for its western engine repair shops. About thirty engines are serviced there regularly. Switchers for this duty are the green and yellow #1011 and #1012 of the Precision National Corporation, an engine-leasing outfit.

The Santa Fe has moved some of its former downtown facilities a short distance to the Hobart Yards at Indiana Street and Washington Boulevard, but heavy repair work has been removed to Barstow. There is a derrick and very old roundhouse in the gray and unused AT & SF shops in San Bernardino (work moved to Barstow). The drabness of the scene is relieved, however, by the presence of the flamboyant, Moorish station, used by the Santa Fe and Amtrak.

A neighbor to the Hobart Yards, just across the Los Angeles River, is the UP's East Los Angeles Yards. Since 1971, the extensive yards have been helped with a hump, to speed the making-up of trains. All heavy work is done in Salt Lake City. The UP (and the AT&SF) put on their Cajon Pass helpers at Colton, off at Summit. I'm told that an occasional sheep wanders over that stretch of track. Poor sheep.

In Los Angeles, many of the old Pacific Electric lines still sprawl over the city like dusty spider webs. They are kept, unused, by the SP, PE's parent, since PE did a good local freight business in addition to their quite famous passenger service.

Remember Mel Blanc, on the Jack Benny show, who regularly implored, "Train leaving on Track 5 for Anaheim, Azusa, and Cu — camonga. Doesn't anybody want to go to Cucamonga?" Guess not. Look what happened to PE. What's more, if you check your map, you'll find that the three towns were all on different PE lines.

Major Roads, San Diego

San Diego, despite its excellent harbor and the intense struggle in the early days among the railroad giants, succeeded in garnering only one major road, the Santa Fe. Its yards are in National City. The old, truncated main line into Elsinore serves only a brickyard and a chemical depot. The station serving the fancy hot springs hotel is a business now, and the tracks are rusting away.

The lack of competition was a real blow to San Diego, until the San Diego & Arizona Eastern was built. It has a minor yard with turntable at 12th and Imperial, San Diego.

Mark Twain (Samuel L. Clemens) (1835-1910):

"It is hard to make railroading pleasant in any country." (1869)

"Traveling with a Reformer" (1893)
"The Railway officials are not aware that there are any kind of insults except spoken ones."

Short Lines

In Los Angeles, there are only two very short lines. The Los Angeles Junction Railroad is three miles of "main line" in Vernon, and sixty-one miles of spurs — between junctions of the SP, UP, and AT&SF. The roundhouse is at Loma Vista and Exchange Streets, housing four units leased from the AT&SF, but none of its own.

The Los Angeles Harbor Railroad is really a paper road. "It" is a joint venture of the UP, SP, and AT&SF to share tracks, begun during World War II, in Los Angeles Harbor. There are dispatchers' offices off Alameda in Wilmington.

Southern Pacific's Mammoth Wharf located at Port Los Angeles as it looked many years ago.

San Diego and Arizona Eastern Railroad, San Diego-El Centro, San Diego and Imperial Counties and Baja California Norte, Mexico

My first visit to the offices of the SD&AE in the old, run-down depot in San Diego revealed a rather unenthusiastic and desultory operation there. I expect the reason was that the line had seen little activity since 1975, when a hurricane took out twenty-five miles of track in the Anza-Borrego Desert.

The SD&AE was John Spreckels' answer to a San Diego need for a direct connection to the East, other than the roundabout Santa Fe route. It eventually came under the control of the SP, which, as a result of the flood, filed for abandonment of nearly the entire line. Fortunately, the ever-present need for public transit rescued the ailing line. The SD&AE is being purchased by the San Diego Metropolitan Transit Development Board for light rail-passenger service as far as the border at San Ysidro.

Moreover, the SP is reconstructing the damage wrought by three years of tropical storms in the desert, prior to turning over the line to the SDMTDB for restored freight service. The SP retains the eastern portion from El Centro to the Plaster City gypsum plant. As a result, San Diego regains its direct freight connection eastward, and the Imperial Valley has its rapid market outlet to the coast.

It is an interesting route. The tracks run into Mexico at Tijuana, where the road is called the Sonora-Baja California Railroad, emerging again into the U.S. at the brewery town of Tecate. From Tecate to Plaster City, a map of the line looks a lot like a diagram of the small intestine, but the grades aren't very steep.

As of this writing, repairs are not yet complete. The SP still operates a daily switcher from El Centro to Plaster City, and two road engines plus a switcher service the branches to El Cajon, Coronado, and fifteen miles of main line south of San Diego. I expect that very soon we'll be seeing the SD&AE logo once again, on its own equipment. There are a few silver-grey work cars in the San Diego yard with SD&AE designation, and in the little hot springs town of Jacumba, half a dozen ancient, wooden commute cars provide homes for the families of some retired trackworkers.

Railroadiana

Museums, Engines, and Cars on Display

Del Mar, San Diego County Fairgrounds. On display, SD&AE #104, 2-8-0 Baldwin Consolidation (1904); John D. Spreckels' private car, SD&AE #050, "Carrizo Gorge" (donated by Railway Historical Society of San Diego).

Lomita, Lomita RR Museum. Replica of a typical station. Inside: history, tickets, buttons, spikes, couplers, whistles, bills, etc. On display: SP #1725, 2-6-0 Baldwin Mogul (1902); boxcar and caboose. Located at 250th and Woodward. Open Wed.-Sun., 10-5, 50¢. (213) 326-6255.

Los Angeles, Travel Town. See description following this list.

Museum of Science and Industry. Located at 700 State Dr. fronting on Univ. of Southern California campus. In transportation section, a huge 750-foot "0" gauge model layout portraying many sections of California. Includes several trains, cars, and planes that forever taxi and never fly. Fare 10¢.

Natural History Museum, at 900 Exposition Blvd. Although it isn't "natural," it is history, and "it" is a streetcar of the Los Angeles Electric Rapid Transit Company (later used on the Pacific Electric) dating back to 1889.

Perris, Orange Empire Railway Museum. See listing under "Rail Rides."

Pomona, Los Angeles County Fairgrounds. Railway & Locomotive Historical Society's "Arcadia Station." Has a museum open during Fair (mid-Sept. to mid-Oct.). On display, many steamers, and a row of giants: Outer Harbor Terminal Ry. (LA) #2, 0-6-0 Schenectady switcher (1887); Fruit Growers Supply Co. #3, three-truck Climax (geared loco) (1909); U.S. Potash Co. #3, 2-8-0 Baldwin (1903), 3' gauge; AT&SF #3450, 4-6-4 Baldwin Hudson (1927); UP #4014, 4-8+8-4 Alco (Schenectady) articulated (1941); SP #5021, 4-10-2 Alco Southern Pacific (1926); UP #9000, 4-12-2 Alco-Brooks Union Pacific (1926); Pacific Electric #1299 Pullman Company "Big Red Car" (1913); AT&SF caboose.

Seal Beach, 8th St. on Electric Ave. On display, PE express baggage car — on old PE right-of-way.

San Diego, Pacific Southwest Railway Museum. On Harbor Dr. waterfront. On display: Coos Bay Lumber Company #11, "John A. Nichols," 2-8-2T Alco Schenectady (1929); AT&SF private car "Victoria." Open 11-5 weekends.

Whaley House, Old Town. On display: San Diego Electric Railway Company #54, standard gauge, California-style trolley (1900s), ex-cable car.

San Bernardino, Viaduct Park. AT&SF #3751, a huge 4-8-4, built in 1927.

Travel Town, Griffith Park, Los Angeles

Founded in 1952 as a transport museum for Los Angeles, the park includes many old cars, fire engines, and airplanes. There has been a one-third mile loop ride on two trolleys. These trolleys have been converted to gasoline, but they are awaiting extensive repair.

Travel Town, Griffith Park, Los Angeles, CA, (213) 661-9465.

On display:

Locomotives, steam: Conrock #1, 0-6-0 Alco Cooke switcher (1925); Stockton Terminal & Eastern #1, 4-4-0 Norris-Lancaster (1864); Camino, Placerville, & Lake Tahoe #2, three-truck Lima Shay (1922), 3′; Pickering Lumber Company #2, two-truck Heisler (1918), ex-Hetch-Hetchy RR; Oahu Sugar Company #5, 0-6-2 Baldwin switcher (1908), 3′; Sharp & Fellows #7, 2-6-2 Alco Dickson Prairie (1902); WP #26, 2-8-0 Alco (Schenectady) Consolidation (1909); LA Harbor Dept. #32, 0-4-0T Alco (Rogers) (1914) (+2 LAHD ore cars); Oahu Ry. #85, 4-6-0 Alco (Cooke) Ten-wheeler (1910), 3′; AT&SF #664, 2-8-0 Baldwin Consolidation (1899); Santa Maria Valley #1000, 2-8-2 Alco Mikado (1920); SP #1273, 0-6-0 SP (Sacramento) (1921); SP #3025, 4-4-2 Baldwin Atlantic (1904), carried Presidents Truman and Roosevelt; UP #4439, 0-6-0 Baldwin switcher (1919).

Interurbans & Trolleys: LA Transit streetcar #536 (1905), "yellow car;" PE #1498 fast freight car (1904); LA Met. Transit Auth. car #1543 (1937?); PE #1544 (1902), ex-North Shore.

Gasoline: AT&SF #M177 track inspection vehicle (1929).

Rolling stock: Passenger cars, SP #4418, SP #2513, SP #3355, UP #LA701, one wooden, one mixed, one UP diner; two cabooses, two boxcars, one tankcar, one Ry. Post Office, one cattlecar, one flatcar.

In storage: S.F. Muni cable car #28; LA Ry. #51 and #57 (now gasoline-powered) awaiting repair; Universal Studios streetcar (c. 1890).

Schedule: 364 days (closed Christmas), 9-5; weekends, 9-5:30.

Fare: Free.

Also: Other antique transport vehicles, picnic facilities, large WC for tour buses, refreshment stand, LA Live Steamers next door.

WHERE THE RAILS OF WRRC MET ON SPANISH CREEK BRIDGE. MORGAN-PHOTO. NOV. 1 1904 63.

Railroadiana, Los Angeles Area

General Phineas T. Banning residence, E. 400 block of Pacific Coast Hwy., Wilmington. Sunday tours of the residence, public use of grounds. Banning (1830-1865) was the builder of San Pedro & LA RR in 1869 and later the LA Harbor. Raised the consciousness of Leland Stanford, who proceeded to buy the road in 1876 for SP's connection to the sea in Los Angeles.

Ford Avenue drawbridge (rail and road) to Terminal Island (1924) is the only one of its kind that exists in Southern California.

Funiculars, at Angel's Flight and Mt. Lowe Ry. have gone (see p. 33), but there is one at Magic Mountain (p. 130).

Huntington Library, 1151 Oxford Rd. San Marino (Pasadena), open year-round except Mondays and the month of October. Railroad material open only to members, not public.

Union Station, downtown. A state historical landmark, a lofty cavern, and a fine example of Art Deco of 1939. Served by Amtrak; owned by SP, UP, and AT&SF.

Universal Studios, Universal City. Things are seldom what they seem — in Hollywood. Tourist buses in this land of illusion suffer a ''near collision'' with old steamer #67. But old #67 is just a mockup with air-driven plastic wheels, canned sound, and oily smoke, and it isn't ''runaway'' at all. Uni-Tour RR #67, 2-8-2 Universal Special Effects (1974), 3' gauge. Close by, but to be seen only from a bus: an old railroad station with three-foot-gauge wooden boxcars (real). (213) 877-1311.

Williams' Train Stop, Electric near Main, Venice. Williams built a train stop on the old Venice PE line to watch for a train that never comes.

A Few Restaurants

''Capistrano Depot,'' San Juan Capistrano. Restored mission-style depot (1895) (AT&SF), still used for Amtrak, is now, augmented by several cars, an elegant eating establishment. Dining room fragrances waft in via an incredible system of four-bladed fans, all belt-driven from a single power source, like a Dickens cotton mill.

''Putney Station,'' 2900 Artesia, Redondo Beach. A sort of Victoria Station.

''McDonalds,'' 510 Central, Glendale. ''Glendale Station.''

''Victoria Station,'' Universal City. A reconstruction of a British Railways station. Inside, schedule board from London's Victoria Station, four cars from the ''Flying Scotsman,'' seen in Hitchcock's early thriller, ''The 39 Steps.'' Also 225-foot funicular from parking lot. Others in Los Angeles, Newport Beach, Torrance, Woodland Hills, and San Diego.

Railfan and Model Clubs

Chula Vista Live Steamers, Rohrer Park, Chula Vista.

Los Angeles Live Steamers, Griffith Park, Los Angeles.

Railway & Locomotive Historical Society, Southern Calif. Chapter, P.O. Box 4068, Pasadena, CA 91106.

Railway Historical Society of San Diego, c/o Gladys Trains Skeen, 4275 University Ave., San Diego.

Balboa Park Model RR Club, meets at the ''House of Charm'' Fri. nights and Sun. (open to public), San Diego.

Model Shops

Los Angeles County

Allied Models, 10938 Pico Blvd., L.A.

Crains Trains & Hobbies, 1112 N. Hacienda Blvd., La Puente.

Display Products Company, (Layouts), 1624 Venice Blvd., L.A.

Railroad Gift Shop, Union Station, 800 N. Alameda, L.A.

Toytown, 8914 Valley, Rosemead.

The Train Master, 13838 Ventura Blvd., Sherman Oaks.

The Train Station, 850 N. Hollywood Way, Burbank.

The Train Stop, 211 W. Bonita, San Dimas.

Troxel Bros. Models, 216 S. Western, L.A.

Washington & Vermont Train Shop, 1583 W. Washington Blvd., L.A.

Western Railroad Novelties, Ltd., 1824 S. Vermont, L.A.

Whistle Stop, 3745 E. Colorado, Pasadena.

Orange & San Bernardino Counties

Barry's Trains, 13071 Euclid, Garden Grove.

End of Track, 630 S. Brea Blvd., Brea.

The Good Life, 14041 Prospect Street, Tustin.

Harper's Hobby Shop, 222 N. G St., San Bernardino.

Hobby City on the Anaheim & Stanton Line, 1238 S. Beach Blvd., Anaheim.

Hobby Junction, 130 E. 9th, Upland.

Mini-Trains, 1113 W. Baker, Costa Mesa.

Train & Hobby Shop, Knott's Berry Farm, Buena Park.

Trans-World Trains, 3121 E. La Palma, Anaheim.

Village Model Shop, 116 W. B. St., Ontario.

San Diego County

Frank the Trainman, 4310 Park Blvd., S.D.

Gladys Trains, 4275 University, S.D.

Jim's Train Depot, 4506 30th St., S.D.

Steam Models & Miniatures

Conway Locomotive, 903 S. Victory, Burbank (model steam).

Little Engines Shop, 2135 250th St., Lomita (coal & oil steam models).

Hurlbut Amusement Company, 7860 Western Ave., Buena Park (larger miniatures).

(Note: If we've missed your model shop and you *specialize* in trains, please let us know.)

The drivers on the trucks of Heislers
are all linked together.

United States Government Railroads

It may come as a surprise to many, but the U.S. Government, in the form of the Department of Defense, has one of the largest and most varied railroad operations in all of California. True, the some 500-600 miles of track are scattered about the various military installations, but over them roll some of the oldest and best-kept diesels in the state. ("The government never throws anything away.") The navy has the most equipment and track — no doubt because of San Francisco, Los Angeles-Long Beach, and San Diego Harbors and several weapons testing stations. But all three services have their share of equipment that shuffles cargo inside their very private gates.

For this book, I have not searched exhaustively for the many tracks and engines currently in use. But in my travels about California, I have come across quite a few. There are still a good many stations at which I have not inquired, and people's willingness to release information has been next to nil. Nevertheless, here is what I have found.

United States Navy

Naval Weapons Station, Concord. Eight specially spark-proofed 126-ton Alco diesels (1953-1955); and about 450 mixed cars on 126 miles of track. Some of the track is on old Bay Point & Clayton roadbed.

Mare Island Naval Station, Vallejo. Two sixty-five-ton GE diesels (1941, 1943); in addition, about fifty-five flatcars and fourteen standard-gauge thirty- to forty-ton rail cranes of 1940s vintage; some thirty miles of track.

Naval Air Station, Alameda. One 1940 GE diesel services their approximately seven miles of track. There is also a twenty-five-ton Colby gantry (1946) with rails 28' 8¼'' apart.

Moffett Field Naval Air Station, Mountain View. Their little diesel switcher has been in disrepair for several years.

Naval Supply Center, Oakland. Has two diesels of WW II vintage, along with twenty flats and several gantrys.

U.S. Navy Support Activity, Long Beach. One Whiting trackmobile (1961) — has both tires and steel wheels.

Naval Weapons Station, Seal Beach. This station has three GE eighty-ton diesels (1953) and some sixty miles of track. Often can be seen working from Hwy. 1 bridge. Incidentally, this station supports a marsh ecology program in the mud flats near the port.

Naval Weapons Station, Fallbrook Annex (to Seal Beach). One eighty-ton GE (1953), on twenty-one miles of track.

Camp Pendleton Marine Base. One GE eighty-ton (1953), and some boxcars and flats, all belonging to Seal Beach Station.

Naval Weapons Center, China Lake. Their two forty-five-ton GE diesels (1944) operate on some nineteen miles of track, some of which was constructed between 1872 and 1888. Also, some oversized and non-standard rolling stock.

Port Hueneme Naval Station, Port Hueneme. Uses one GE diesel (1953) and a few tank cars. Connects to the Ventura County Ry. Nearby is the Seabees Museum, with artifacts mostly of WW II vintage in the Pacific theater.

USMC Supply Center, Yermo. "Two old diesels on a few miles of track."

United States Army

Oakland Army Base, Oakland. Its diesels, #1856, 120-ton Fairbanks-Morse (1952) and #1269, 60-ton Baldwin-Lima-Hamilton (1954) shuttle cars over about forty miles of track.

Sharp Army Depot, Stockton. Uses two sixty-ton Baldwins (1953) over its forty miles of track, along with two Ford track-inspection motor cars. Several other engines in storage.

Sierra Ordnance Depot, Susanville. One diesel, several miles of track.

United States Air Force

Travis AFB, Fairfield, Has an eighty-ton GE for its few miles of track.

Note: Many stations, especially army and air force, now use specially constructed trucks for transportation of equipment, and pipelines for transport of aviation fuel. The tracks to and within these stations still exist, but are unused.

Supplement and Bibliography

The following are additional steam locomotives donated by the Southern Pacific for public display. These were taken from a listing; I have not actually seen these engines and therefore cannot comment on their present location.

Alameda, *Washington Park*, #1227, 0-6-0 Lima (1915).

Bloomington, *San Bernardino County Museum.* #2824, 2-8-0 Brooks (1908).

Hanford, Kings County, *Burris Park*, #1215, 0-6-0 Baldwin (1913).

Martinez, Contra Costa County, *City Park*, #1258, 0-6-0 Southern Pacific (Los Angeles shops) (1921).

Monterey, *El Estero Park*, #1285, 0-6-0 Lima (1924).

Oakland, Alameda County, Auditorium, CP #233, 2-6-2T Central Pacific (Sacramento shops) (1882).

Orland, Glenn County, *Fairgrounds*, #2852, 2-8-0 Southern Pacific (Sacramento) (1919).

Richmond, Contra Costa County, *Nicholl Park*, #1269, 0-6-0 SP (Sacramento) (1921).

Roseville, Placer County, *Fairgrounds*, #2252, 4-6-0 Cooke (1897).

Salinas, Monterey County, *Central Park*, #1237, 0-6-0 Baldwin (1918).

San Jose, Santa Clara County, *Fairgrounds*, #2479, 4-6-2 Baldwin (1923).

San Mateo, *County Fairgrounds*, #2472, 4-6-2 Baldwin (1921).

Stockton, San Joaquin County, *Junior Museum*, #1251, 0-6-0 SP (Sacramento) (1919).

Tracy, San Joaquin County, *Dr. Powers Park*, #1293, 0-6-0 Lima (1924).

Watsonville, Santa Cruz County, *Ramsey Park*, #2706, 2-8-0 Baldwin (1904).

Woodland, Yolo County, *Fairgrounds*, #1233, 0-6-0 Baldwin (1918).

May I also mention that there are a number of private corporation yards with locomotives in use (and some on display). These yards, like some of the lumber companies, are not really *railroad* companies, but they certainly do have rails, engines, and often very specialized equipment.

In this category I would list General American Tank Car Corp. (whose cars bear the designation "GATX"), and whose yards are in West Colton, on Pepper Ave. On display there is the retired #65-1, a 1937 0-4-0 Plymouth with Buda gasoline power. Working in the yards are #65990, a Baldwin-Lima-Hamilton-built 35-ton Whitcomb, and #RE 1014, a leased 110-ton Alco.

Here also goes the big fleet of Kaiser Steel engines at their Fontana Works (most data unavailable), ranging from the #8178 donkey to #32-002, a hump-yard switcher. There are many miles of track at this huge plant, and it is a real pleasure to watch the multitude of tasks that their engines perform.

This category includes, too, the very pretty engine belonging to Foster Farms' elevators and chicken ranch in Livingston (on Hwy. 99, near Merced).

For future editions, I'd appreciate any input, with details, from fans or companies wishing to see other engines or rail operations in this category.

An artist's conception of crossing the country by immigrant train in the old days.

Books

Burby, John. *The Great American Motion Sickness, or Why You Can't Get There from Here*. Boston: Little, Brown & Co., 1971.

Crump, Spencer. *Redwoods, Iron Horses, and the Pacific*. Los Angeles: Trans-Anglo Books, 1963. History of the California Western RR.

Daggett, Stuart. *Chapters on the History of the Southern Pacific*. New York: Ronald Press Co., 1922.

Davis, Olive. *The Slow, Tired, & Easy RR*. Fresno: Valley Publishers, 1976. History of the Stockton Terminal & Eastern RR.

Duke, Donald, and Kistler, Stan. *Santa Fe — Steel Rails Through California*. San Marino: Golden West Books, 1964.

Hilton, George W. *The Cable Car in America*. Berkeley: Howell-North, 1971.

Holbrook, Stewart. *The Story of American Railroads*. New York: Crown Publishers, 1947.

Hungerford, John. *The Slim Princess*. Reseda: Hungerford Press, 1961. History of the Southern Pacific Narrow Gauge Keeler Branch and the Carson & Colorado RR.

Johnston, Hank. *Railroads of the Yosemite Valley*. Long Beach: Johnston-Howe Publications, 1963.

Kneiss, Gilbert. *Bonanza Railroads*. Palo Alto: Stanford University Press, 1946. Descriptive histories of smaller California and Nevada railroads.

Kneiss, Gilbert. *Redwood Railways*. Berkeley: Howell-North, 1956. Histories of the North Pacific Coast RR, the Northwestern Pacific RR, their predecessors, and neighboring lines.

McAfee, Ward. *California Railroads, 1850-1911*. San Marino: Golden West Books, 1973.

Myrick, David. *Railroads of Nevada and Eastern California*. Vols. 1 and 2. Berkeley: Howell-North, 1962. Excellent, exhaustive history of this region.

Polkinghorn, R.S. *Pino Grande,* Berkeley: Howell-North, 1966. Includes history of the Camino, Placerville, & Lake Tahoe RR.

Puckett, Howard. *A Guide to Fun Railroads of the West*. Santa Rosa: Howard Puckett Promotions, 1977.

Sebree, Mac, and Walker, Jim. *Where Travel Means the Trolley*. Perris: Orange Empire Trolley Museum, 1970. A guidebook to the Orange Empire Railway Museum.

Tenney, Will, and Reynolds, Richard. *California Railway Museum*. Rio Vista Jct.: Bay Area Electric RR Association. A guidebook to the museum.

Tompkins, Walter. *Mattei's Tavern — Where Road Met Rail in Stagecoach Days*. Santa Barbara: Walter Tompkins, 1974.

Wagner, Jack. *Short Line Junction*. Fresno: Academy Library Guild, 1956. Histories of several California and Nevada short lines.

Walsh, Peggy. *Yreka Western Milestones*. Yreka: Western RR, 1966.

Whitaker, Rogers, and Hiss, Anthony. *All Aboard With E.M. Frimbo, World's Greatest Railroad Buff*. New York: Viking, 1974.

Wurm Theodore, and Graves, Alvin. *The Crookedest Railroad in the World*. Berkeley: Howell-North, 1960. History of the Mill Valley & Mt. Tamalpais RR.

"IER — The Big Red Cars," 1966; "Market Street Railway, 1934-1944," 1961-1962; "San Francisco Municipal Railway, 1912-1944," 1965, 1961, 1968. All published by Western Railroader, San Mateo, Francis A. Guido, Publisher.

Index

Subject

Notes

Notes

Notes